P9-CSF-840

The Harvard Business School

Guide to Finding Your Next Job

The Harvard Business School

Guide to Finding Your Next Job

Robert S. Gardella

Harvard Business Reference

Boston, Massachusetts

Copyright 2000 President and Fellows of Harvard College
All rights reserved
Printed in the United States of America
04 03 02 01 00 5 4 3 2 1

Library of Congress Cataloging-in-Publication Data

Gardella, Robert S., 1946–
    The Harvard Business School guide to finding your next
      job / Robert S. Gardella.
      p.   cm.
    Includes bibliographical references and index.
    ISBN 1-57851-223-9
    1. Job hunting--United States--Handbooks, manuals, etc.
  2. Vocational guidance--United States--Handbooks, manuals,
etc. I. Title: Guide to finding your next job. II. Title: Finding
your next job. III. Title.

HF5382.75.U6 G37 2000
650.14--dc21   99-058454

The paper used in this publication meets the requirements
of the American National Standard for Permanence of Paper
for Publications and Documents in Libraries and Archives
Z39.48-1992.

To the "Big Three"—my mother, Mary (Harrington) Gardella, and her two surviving siblings, my aunts Fran Ryding and Betty Manning. The emotional and financial support that each of you has provided through my personal and career transitions has been tremendous. I'm sure there are spots reserved in heaven for the three of you—next to one another, naturally.

Contents

Preface

I HAVE LONG BEEN A FAN of handouts, both as a student and a professional trainer. This book, in fact, began life as a handout. In late 1992, a successful job seeker sent me a two-page compilation of job-search tips, "Getting a Job Is Challenging Work," that he also sent to the rest of the network he had established. I liked its advice and its straightforward approach and used it for a couple of years in my work as an outplacement counselor and trainer. It inspired me to begin developing a more comprehensive collection of job-search tips that I called "Things to Keep in Mind in Your Job Search."

While counseling at career centers established for groups of managers, professionals, and other workers being "outplaced" from specific firms, I began writing and editing newsletter articles on various aspects of the search process. Preparing them helped me to put down on paper the ideas I was using in job-search workshops and one-on-one counseling. I later combined this material and "Things to Keep in Mind in Your Job Search" into one document explaining and amplifying my views on the overall job-search process, but retaining the basic approach from "Getting a Job Is Challenging Work."

In the fall of 1996, I delivered a session for the Acton/Boxboro/Stow, Massachusetts, job-search support group structured around the document that I then thought was complete at fourteen pages. After that session, however, I kept coming across good job-search "to-do" lists and thinking about other ideas worth incorporating and better ways to explain job-search concepts. Working on the document became almost a hobby—my wife, Judi, would say an obsession. But I also continued to use it in my work, and the text slowly evolved with a lot of valuable input, and overwhelmingly positive feedback, from a wide variety of people.

Although originally geared toward experienced people who are out of work, the book's advice applies to any job seeker at any point in his or her career. For example, recent college graduates, or those soon to graduate, will find specific advice tailored to them. In addition, feedback from Harvard Business School alumni around the world has convinced me that the job-search process everywhere has become more "Americanized." So, although this book was written about the job search in the United States, most of its advice applies to the search process in other countries.

Acknowledgments

SPECIAL THANKS to Reo Hamel, with whom I served on the steering committee of the Acton/Boxboro/Stow, Massachusetts, job-search support group for more than six years and worked full-time for a year and then later on shorter consulting assignments. He taught me a great deal about the search process and reassured me that my gut instincts on job-search issues are usually on target. The commonsense approach that Reo uses in workshops and one-on-one counseling (documented in *The Next Step*, an outplacement manual he co-authored with Frank McCarthy) has been a significant influence on my work.

Thanks to two career and entrepreneurial advisers with whom I worked and from whom I learned. Ellie Byers is a career counselor with whom I co-managed a Drake Beam Morin (DBM) Career Center for former Vermont employees of Digital Equipment Corporation. Tina Kerkam, Senior Vice President of Studley & Associates, had worked for DBM and with me at the DBM/Stratus Computer Transition Support Center before joining her current firm.

Thanks also go to a number of other people who contributed in various ways to the development of this book:

Greg Enos, for creating and sending me "Getting a Job Is Challenging Work" and starting me on this path.

Ed Alexander, Kathy Mahler, Susan Meyers, Jurg Oppliger, and Bob Woodhouse, the 1994–95 IBM/DBM Career Center consulting team in Vermont, for reviewing my initial articles for that center's weekly newsletter and commenting on my first attempt at expanding "Getting a Job Is Challenging Work."

Carolyn Andrews, Penny Dunning, Michele Murray, Joyce Santello, Claire Snow-Posterro, Linda Woods, and Christine (MacLellan) Yeomans, the outstanding staff of the 1995–96 Stratus Computer outplacement project (in addition to Tina Kerkam), and Rich Marciante, the Stratus project leader, for supporting and encouraging me as I expanded and articulated my ideas in that center's biweekly newsletter.

Elaine Sullivan, who worked with me on the DBM/Polymer Technology outplacement project, for reviewing two versions of the book and making a number of excellent suggestions; and Gail Liebhaber, for suggesting that I strengthen the material on transition issues and the emotional aspects of the job search.

Ron Bloch, Gary Couch, and Kris Girrell, all former DBM consultants, for ideas from their separate written handouts on job fairs.

Fred Studley, a speaker at the November 1996 session of the Acton/Boxboro/Stow, Massachusetts, job-search group, for the excellent job-search ideas he shared at that session.

Neil MacKenna, a veteran job-search counselor and Harvard Business School (HBS) alumnus, for sharing his philosophy of and approach to the job search and providing me with a great deal of helpful feedback.

Akie Kondo, my office manager at the HBS Office of Alumni Career Services, for finding a number of typos and awkward phrases that had crept into the document over time, and Christine Fairchild, HBS Director of Alumni Relations, for reviewing and critiquing the document.

Mary Stark, an executive search consultant, for information about the compensation of contingency search firms; and Pam Huntington, another search professional and an HBS alumna, for reviewing the revised search firm section.

Jon Winder, Senior Vice President at Harvard Business School Publishing, for bringing my manuscript to the Harvard Business School Press; and Claudia Bruce, my editor at the Press, for making the restructuring and editing suggestions that helped me shape the document into a book.

Alan Hutchings of the HBS on-campus copy center, for producing many copies, thus helping me to "get the word out" to a large number of people.

Jed Bullard, former Vice President of the HBS Alumni Board and former chair of its Career Management Committee, for his enthusiastic support of my work in general and of this book in particular.

Rickie Moriarty, Director of Boston's Operation ABLE, for reviewing and commenting on the "Overcoming Age Discrimination" section in Chapter 7.

Barbara Sutton, my Harvard Business School Press copy editor, for very effectively rewording and clarifying the final draft manuscript.

Finally, thanks to:

The thousands of Harvard Business School alumni, outplacement candidates from numerous companies, and other job seekers with whom I have worked, for sharing their lives and job-search dilemmas with me.

A variety of friends and network contacts, for reading earlier versions of this text and providing a great deal of constructive feedback: Bob Armstrong, Jack Falvey, Leslie Gabriele, Roberta Goldschmidt, Tom Gorman, Pam Lassiter, Helene Lauer, Ken Lizotte, Donna Maltzan, Lesley Wong Mancini, Kirsten Moss, Laura Powers, Sydney Rice-Harrild, Clarissa Sawyer, John Tovrov, and Michael Wertheim.

And to my wife, Judi Hess, recruiter extraordinaire, who ignores most of the advice given here but finds a job anyway. She is living proof of my conviction that, in the job-search process, all advice must be adapted to the individual and the situation.

Introduction

SEARCHING FOR A JOB is one of the most important things that professionals do, and they are doing it much more frequently. The changing employer/employee contract, the lack of job security, the increasing pace of change in the workplace, advances in technology, globalization, and even the quest for a better work/life balance are all creating significant movement in the marketplace for jobs. Another prominent factor has been the overall strength of the U.S. economy since the recession in the early 1990s. People are changing jobs because of the opportunities that have been created and, for some, because of the fear that they will miss out on opportunities now available.

Although the job search is a crucially important process for most professionals, it is also one of the most feared, misunderstood, and mishandled activities, even by otherwise intelligent, accomplished people. The good news is that you can get better at this process.

Let me start with a simple but powerful, and I hope empowering, concept: There is only one answer to almost all job-search questions— "it depends."

"IT DEPENDS" IS THE ANSWER

Searching for a job is an art, not a science; there are few absolutes. Everything depends on the individual and the situation. This point has been demonstrated repeatedly to me in working with thousands of job seekers at widely varying employment levels over the past decade.

Although the job search is an art, there are effective search methodologies and approaches; most are applications of common sense. They often reflect the Golden Rule—doing unto others as you would have them do unto you. You also need to consider how any job-search action you take might be perceived at the receiving end.

A few years ago, a friend of mine found a book on this topic that was published in 1937. The book did not mention faxing your résumé, having it scanned in, or surfing the Internet for jobs, but most of its advice was still valid sixty years later.

People often have problems applying search methods because of the emotional component involved. It is hard to be "objective" when your life, career, and future seem to be at stake. Some job seekers overlook, or don't seem to fully appreciate, that the search process is both an intellectual *and* an emotional one.

The job search also is a marketing and sales process, and most job seekers are not experienced with, or comfortable in, those disciplines. And even those who are experienced in these areas—people who find it easy to market a specific product or service—often have difficulty applying these disciplines to their own search.

There are no magic bullets in the search process. Determination, effort, patience, perseverance, timing, and luck all can play key roles in your eventual success. Many job seekers hope to find one or two things they can do to guarantee getting a job or their dream job. There are no guarantees, unless you start or buy a business. You will have a job, but only if your business prospers.

Anything you do in the job search, no matter how many sources recommend it, will make a good impression on some and not on others. It is highly unlikely that you can "do the right thing" for everyone you encounter in your search. Your goal is to impress those people you might want to work for or with, who might lead you to a job or offer other help in your search. Be yourself in the job search, but be sure it is your best possible self.

Adapt all job-search advice to your own personality, style, and approach. Ignore advice that does not work for you, but don't avoid the tougher tasks in job search, such as contacting strangers or near strangers. The real applicability of the "it depends" concept comes in how you understand and apply the ideas and techniques found in how-to books like this one and in many other books, articles, Internet sites, and job-search resources, as well as those suggested by friends, network contacts, career counselors, and outplacement consultants.

A Harvard Business School alumna whom I helped in mid-1998 was doing her first post-HBS job search, leaving a company involuntarily after twenty years. Perhaps she said it best: "People give all sort of suggestions and advice [in the job search], some aspects of which appear to be at odds with others. The individual's responsibility is to sort it all out and to determine what to do given the circumstances. 'It depends' is a little scary at the beginning (if I really knew already, I wouldn't ask) but is liberating and even empowering as I go on (after my ego bounces back and starts functioning as a problem-solver again)."

BUT NETWORKING IS KEY

The bottom line in the job search is that most people find jobs through friends, relatives, colleagues, classmates, and other acquaintances (by networking). It was true in the past, is true now, and will be for the foreseeable future, despite the apparent belief of some that searching for a job over the Internet is fundamentally changing the search process. Networking is not the only way to find a job, but statistically it is by far the most effective technique. And the higher you go in organizations, the more important it becomes.

This book makes a wide variety of suggestions for how to be your best possible self throughout the search process. Become a student of this process. Learn and implement effective job-search methods, and build a personal network to help you now and in the future. Given current economic predictions, you will be looking for a job again and probably sooner and much more often than you would prefer.

The Harvard Business School

Guide to Finding Your Next Job

1

Getting Started

EVERYONE WHO CHANGES JOBS needs to start the job-search process somewhere. Whether you are looking for your next position voluntarily or because your current one has been or is being eliminated, you will go through a series of steps on your way to your next job. This book focuses on the process of finding a new job, not of changing careers. But even career changers, once they define what they want to do, will have to find jobs, so this book can help them, too.

This opening chapter describes how to begin, providing special advice for those who left their last job involuntarily and for those who are seeking new careers.

PREPARING FOR THE JOB SEARCH

Inventory your skills, knowledge, interests, experiences, and job (and nonwork) preferences. Who are you, what have you done, what are you good at, what do you like to do (and want to do next), and what do you want to avoid? More important, how can you best help hiring managers solve specific problems? The people who do that best are the ones who get hired.

As you ask yourself those key questions, don't think about "what you want to do when you grow up." Concentrate instead on "what you want to do next," perhaps something that will better position you for attaining your ultimate career goal. Try to define your ideal next job (or jobs) and your work preferences in terms of a variety of aspects such as industry, location, work environment, level of responsibility, commuting and travel requirements, company profile and culture, type of supervisor, company size, and pre- or post-IPO status.

If your recent work has not been satisfying, use this transition as an opportunity to take a broad look at all the possibilities. Consider your options for changing careers, for instance, or for becoming an entrepreneur or for achieving a better balance between your work life and your personal life.

For new or recent college graduates, perhaps the most critical thing is the manager or supervisor you will work for. Finding a supervisor who enjoys, knows how to work with, and wants to develop new talent may be even more important than closely matching your job preferences.

Take advantage of the numerous self-assessment devices available, but be cautious when interpreting and applying the results. No assessment instrument can tell you what profession you should be in or even what you should do next. The results from several, however, can increase your self-awareness, show your career aptitudes and trends, and help you avoid potential mismatches.

Learn about each self-assessment device and the information it can and can't provide. After you complete each one, get help interpreting the results, if you feel it is necessary, from career or outplacement consultants or organizations that administer and interpret the devices. Look for themes—tendencies or trends across results from multiple devices.

Perhaps the best-known vocational self-assessment instrument is the Strong Interest Inventory. This well-respected device has been used for a number of years. You may have taken it in high school or college, when it was known as the Strong-Campbell Interest Inventory. It assesses your interests against those typically associated with a wide range of careers. It might tell you, for instance, that you have interests similar to those of business executives, forest rangers, and police officers.

The Myers-Briggs Type Indicator (MBTI) is a widely used personality assessment instrument. Although it is often called on to help people improve their interpersonal communication skills by identifying their MBTI personality "type" (one of sixteen), it also has career applications. For additional information, read one or more of the following books:

- *Do What You Are: Discover the Perfect Career for You Through the Secrets of Personality Type,* by Paul D. Tieger and Barbara Barron-Tieger

- *Type Talk at Work,* by Otto Kroeger and Janet Thuesen

- *Work Types,* by Jean M. Kummerov, Nancy J. Barger, and Linda K. Kirby

The Business Career Interest Inventory (BCII) is a tool designed for those focusing on careers in business. In *Discovering Your Career in Business,* Timothy Butler and James Waldroop describe the inventory; the book includes a diskette that allows you to complete the instrument on a PC. You can find additional information about the BCII on the authors' Web site at <www.careerdiscovery.com>. When you visit that site, you may want to take a free guided tour of *CareerLeader,* a Web-based self-assessment service that integrates the BCII with two additional devices—a rewards profile and a skills assessment tool.

Another potentially useful Web site is <www.futurestep.com>. Futurestep, a company funded by the executive search firm Korn/Ferry International and *The Wall Street Journal,* provides an on-line job matching service for people in the $75K–$250K salary range. The on-line registration process includes completion of a free self-assessment device similar to *CareerLeader.* The results, provided within twenty-four hours, include your "estimated salary market value."

COPING WITH JOB LOSS

Avoid rushing into a job search before you are prepared, particularly if you recently lost your job. Although the early stages of the search process feature a number of set tasks, give yourself a few days or even a week or more, if possible, to get grounded. This advice might not seem, or be, practical if you have significant financial pressures or if any outplacement services provided by your former employer are time-limited. Still, most of those recently laid off do take the time to get their bearings, whether they plan to or not.

An excellent pamphlet that suggests appropriate strategies and tactics for the initial period of job loss is *The Benefits of Being Laid Off,* by Priscilla Claman with Scott Carson. Privately published, it is available through Claman's Boston-based firm, Career Strategies, Inc. (617-227-5517, or via e-mail at <careerstra@aol.com>; the Web site is <www.career-strategies.com>).

Don't think of yourself as "tainted" if you are out of work. Given today's turbulent business environment, the only social stigma associated with unemployment is the one you put on yourself (as some losing their jobs still do). Because so many workers at all levels have been directly affected by downsizing, mergers, reorganizations, and the many business changes since the late 1980s—an estimated 10 percent of the working population—your employment status *usually* is not an issue with hiring managers. These managers are more concerned that you have the skills and experience to meet their organization's needs and to solve its problems; their focus is likely to be on current rather than long-term needs.

Realize that any negative feelings you have about losing your job are normal. Try not to dwell on these feelings, but be reasonable with yourself: You may not adapt to your new status as quickly as you thought you would.

Put your last job (and organization) behind you. Resentments about the past do not help your efforts to create a new future. In particular, avoid being perceived by others as a complainer.

If you feel stuck, William Bridges's *Transitions* (first published by Addison-Wesley in 1980; now available in paperback from Perseus Books) may help. Although not about job search per se, the book provides an excellent discussion of "endings," "new beginnings," and the uncomfortable but critically important "neutral zone" in between. Seeds planted in the neutral zone often flourish in the new beginning.

Don't be surprised if your emotional reaction to job loss is serious enough to warrant professional psychiatric help. Most surveys find that job loss—along with divorce and the death of a child, a spouse, or a parent—is at or near the top of the scale of life stressors. Individual, couples, or family counseling may be appropriate. Job loss can put a tremendous strain on an individual's relationship with a partner or spouse or with his or her family.

After losing a job, answer these questions about your employer:

1. **What did your employer tell you?** (The "official" version.)

2. **What do you believe?** (What you really think happened.)

3. **What are you going to tell people?** (Anyone you speak with, but particularly potential interviewers.)

Then, forget your answers to the first two questions and concentrate on your direct and concise answer to Question 3, which, if possible, includes positive statements about your former company and even your former supervisor. Even if you left your previous job voluntarily (or are doing a job search while still employed), use the preceding sequence of questions to devise a reasoned and reasonable response to the inevitable "Why are you on the job market?" question.

Schedule in "worry time." Because anger, fear, frustration, and similar emotions are natural components of the job-search process, especially when you are out of work, why not make them part of your schedule? Worry for two specified hours each week, then ignore these concerns the rest of the time. This intriguing idea, adapted from *The Next Step,* by Frank McCarthy and Reo Hamel, is probably impossible to implement, but keeping it in mind might make the emotional components of losing a job and looking for a new one somewhat easier to cope with.

FINANCIAL CONSIDERATIONS

Review your assets and liabilities and then devise ways to eliminate unnecessary expenses. The job-search process will be easier if you are not worrying about whether you will have enough money to get by. One of the first questions I often ask people who are in or considering a job transition is "How long could you last [financially]?" A person who answers "two or more years" can consider a much different search strategy from the person who answers "one to two months."

Develop and maintain a budget. Be realistic about the limitations of your financial situation but be sure to factor in occasional treats— your job search will be hard work, and rewarding yourself here and there will contribute to your emotional well-being.

Plan for a lengthy search but hope for (and work toward) a short one. Building momentum in a job search takes time (think of it as a process rather than an event.) No matter how hard you work at this process, factors such as the strength of the overall job market and the availability of opportunities in your field or geographic area are going to be out of your control.

Check out the books, articles, and other resources aimed at helping you save money while in transition. Two good books to consider are: *1001 Ways to Cut Your Expenses,* by Jonathan Pond, and *Surviving Unemployment,* by Cathy Beyer, Doris Pike, and Loretta McGovern.

Those who want to use this period to reconsider their overall approach to money will find *Your Money or Your Life: Transforming Your Relationship with Money and Achieving Financial Independence,* by Joe Dominguez and Vicki Robin, useful. *The Millionaire Next Door: The Surprising Secrets of America's Wealthy,* by Thomas J. Stanley and William D. Danko, will help to dispel some of the myths about wealth accumulation and who is "wealthy" in the United States.

Find out about government-sponsored programs to help those out of work. In addition to unemployment compensation, the jobless can benefit from federal retraining funds and free or discounted medical coverage in some states. Be willing to accept these funds or take advantage of available programs. Companies you have worked for have been paying into the unemployment insurance system during your work life; now you need the system to help you while you attempt to re-enter the job market.

Contact all your creditors and try to negotiate payment schedules that comply with your budget. Mortgage holders and credit card companies often are willing to make special arrangements for their customers, but you must notify them early on and keep them informed of your employment status.

Track job-search expenses for income tax purposes. A variety of items are deductible (for instance, long-distance phone calls, travel and transportation expenses, typing and mailing of résumés), but only if they are related to your job search, documented, and over a certain percentage of your adjusted gross income. If you plan to deduct your job-search expenses, you must keep detailed records and be looking for a job that is similar to your previous occupation. The federal government does not seem to favor new graduates or career changers. And remember that, although income taxes are typically not withheld from unemployment compensation, you are required to pay tax on this compensation.

CONSIDERING A CAREER CHANGE

Be realistic if you are looking to change careers or to pursue a job in a different industry. You may have many good reasons for exploring a field or an industry in which your credentials and experience may not be particularly relevant or may not seem immediately applicable. If you have been unsatisfied with your recent work or if the demand for your current profession or home industry is on the decline, you certainly have the incentive to look elsewhere.

Although career changes are occurring more frequently, they are harder to make because an organization's hiring manager is typically looking for someone to walk in and deliver on the first day; employers assume that they will not have to train the candidate or allot him or her any start-up time. On the other hand, economic forecasters believe that most Americans will go through three to four (or more) careers in their lifetimes. (I consider this dichotomy one of the great paradoxes in current job-search and overall career management.)

Balance your desire and enthusiasm for change against the realities of the job market and the significant effort that changing careers requires. To change careers, you will have to work very hard—probably much harder than the typical job seeker. Concentrate initially on determining what you might want to do and eliminating areas in which you have no interest. Test the feasibility of your ideas in the marketplace, and then narrow your focus, plan your strategies, and organize your tools. Changing careers probably will take a tremendous amount of time and effort.

Do field research. Cover letters, résumés, and phone calls alone are usually not enough to sell yourself in a new career. Be prepared to get in front of people, and as many people as possible in networking meetings, also called "informational interviews" or even better termed "field research" meetings. People need to see the spark in your eye to determine if they are willing to take a chance on you.

As the interviewer (yes, you are in charge) at a field research meeting, you can ask many questions, but three general questions and the responses to them can fill up a half-hour, hour-long, or even longer session:

1. Ask the person with whom you are meeting about his or her career history to get the person talking and thus learn more about the industry, discipline, company, and so forth. This approach will also give you the opportunity to make "connections" with *your* background and experience.

2. Ask for feedback on your career-change strategy (or suggestions for a strategy if you have yet to develop one, which is perfectly acceptable early in the career-change process).

3. Near the end of the session, ask for suggestions of others with whom you could speak to obtain more information about the industry, discipline, company, and so on. (Get networking referrals.)

If you asked for twenty minutes of the individual's time when you set up the appointment, then at eighteen or nineteen minutes, remind the person that the time you asked for is almost up. Let him or her say that it is okay to keep going but be prepared to stop if he or she does not. Follow up on each field research meeting with the near-mandatory thank-you letter (or an e-mail message), then keep these people informed about your career-change process. Those you meet are now part of your personal network.

If you think it critical to meet face-to-face with someone who is too busy to see you at his or her office, invite that person to breakfast, lunch, or dinner. (Plan to pay, and at least offer to do so.) If you opt for breakfast (often the best choice these days), find out where the person lives and works, and suggest meeting somewhere in between.

Think in terms of income flow(s) rather than salary. You may need, or want, to start work in a new field or industry on a temporary basis.

Be prepared for emotional upheaval. Although career change has become much more common (and more socially acceptable) than it was even a decade ago, it still requires a significant emotional adjustment. An analogy has been made to "shedding your skin" and growing new skin—clearly the process has its discomforts.

Review some of the many helpful books on career change. Numerous guides have been published to help you navigate the challenging process of changing careers.

Richard Bolles's *What Color Is Your Parachute?*, republished yearly, is the best-selling career and job-changing book of all time. A thoroughly entertaining text, *Parachute* contains many insightful and effective pencil-and-paper (i.e., not computerized) self-assessment exercises. Many people have bought and read this book, but fewer have completed the time-consuming and intellectually and emotionally difficult exercises or analyzed the results. Although suggestions for analysis are offered, the task is nonetheless daunting for most people.

Another popular book is *In Transition* (first published in 1991), by Mary Lindley Burton and Richard A. Wedemeyer, which contains more than twenty excellent pencil-and-paper self-assessment exercises. With its practical, businesslike approach to the job search and the career changing process, the text continues to be timely.

Other good books on this topic include:

- *Making a Living While Making a Difference: A Guide to Creating Careers with a Conscience,* by Melissa Everett

- *Doing the Work You Love: Discovering Your Purpose and Realizing Your Dreams,* by Cheryl Gilman

- *Love Your Work and Success Will Follow,* by Arlene Hirsch

- *Life Work Transitions.com: Putting Your Spirit Online,* by Deborah L. Knox and Sandra S. Butzel

- *Wishcraft: How to Get What You Really Want; I Could Do Anything If I Only Knew What It Was: How to Discover What You Really Want and How to Get It; Live the Life You Love;* and *It's Only Too Late If You Don't Start Now: How to Create Your Second Life at Any Age,* all four by Barbara Sher

- *Do What You Love, the Money Will Follow* and *To Build the Life You Want, Create the Work You Love,* both by Marsha Sinetar

2

References

ALTHOUGH REFERENCES can be extremely important in the job search, job seekers can easily put off choosing them and lining them up—perhaps because references are not usually contacted until just before a job offer is made. Some employment agencies and search firms, however, may want to check your references up front, before deciding if they will represent you. It is critical to establish your references early in the search process.

Some might question the importance of references, as organizations normally refuse to furnish references for current or past employees (because of the fear of lawsuits), and reference checkers expect that the individuals you choose will present you in the best light. In one sense, then, having good references might not seem to help you significantly, given that potential employers will generally expect this of you. Still, a negative or lukewarm reference is likely to doom your candidacy.

If you carefully select and then communicate with the people you want to use as references, you won't have to worry about being "torpedoed" by one of them. And remember that these individuals can be extremely helpful in your networking efforts and other aspects of your job search.

SELECTING REFERENCES

Pick your references carefully and early; make finalizing them one of your first job-search tasks. References are a precious resource; you

should protect them, nurture them, and keep them informed. If someone is willing to write a letter of reference for you, thank him or her
and accept the letter (even offer to prepare the initial draft), but also
ask if this person would accept phone calls from your potential
employers. Although written letters of references might be helpful
(and are required in academia and some other fields), most reference
checks are done now by phone.

For higher-level positions, the reference-checking process is likely
to be more informal—perhaps done over a drink, at the gym, or at a
social event. For most job seekers, however, the more standard reference procedures described in this chapter apply, so you need to understand and prepare for them.

*Choose three to six (or more) people who know you well, primarily
from work settings if you are a job seeker with work experience.* The
distinction between "professional" and "personal" references is less
clear than it used to be. Although most of your references will come
from your professional life, they might actually be personal references, as many organizations refuse to provide formal references for
former employees (and don't want their managers to do so). In other
words, it is now the norm for references you are using because of a
work experience to be representing themselves rather than their
employer.

Consider these guidelines in selecting references:

- Choose managers or supervisors with whom you had regular
  contact—people who can speak about your job performance.
  Although the inclusion of a CEO, a company president, or some
  other high-level executive might seem to strengthen your case,
  consider how difficult it will be for the reference checker to
  speak to such a person. The more difficult it is to connect with a
  reference, the less likely the person will be contacted (unless the
  reference checker decides that the specified person's input is
  essential to the hiring decision).

- Include peers or project co-workers. If you are seeking a managerial or supervisory position, include one or more direct reports.

- Consider customers or clients, whether internal or external to
  your current or previous organization(s). Vendor personnel are
  also a possibility. (If you are currently employed, however, be
  extremely careful about asking someone from these groups, as
  this choice might adversely affect your job.)

- Don't rule out people who are retired, between jobs, or working as independent consultants. Although at least some of your references should be currently employed, their employment status is not as important as their knowledge of your experience, attributes, and contributions.

- Consider those with whom, or for whom, you work or have worked in a volunteer capacity in professional, community, sports, or other activities.

- Include academic references (college professors and administrators), especially if you have strong, ongoing relationships with individuals from your academic experiences. Such references are particularly appropriate if you are about to complete, or have recently completed, an academic program.

Although you also can choose someone from your personal life as a reference, and you occasionally may be asked for personal as well as professional references, reference checkers normally want people who can address your work activities, performance, style, and accomplishments.

For those out of work, include your last manager or supervisor if possible. If that person will not be a good reference, leave him or her out; be prepared to explain why the person is not included, but only if someone asks.

Ask the people you select if they are willing to serve as a reference; don't just assume that they will. If they are willing,

- give them your résumé (and any subsequent major updates).

- inform them of the kind of position(s) you are looking for and any other major search criteria.

- provide them with any list(s) you have, or later develop, of organizations you plan to target in your search. (Your references might know someone at one or more of these firms.)

- give them any additional information that you think would help them to support your candidacy (but don't overwhelm them with material).

- coach them about their work experience with you. Remind former managers/supervisors, particularly those from the somewhat distant past, of when and how long you worked for them, what your position or title was, what your primary responsibilities were, and what you did well for them.

Determine where (at work or at home) and at what time your references would prefer to be called. They might not have a preference. Either day or evening availability is acceptable, although it is probably better that your references be accessible during the day. Both day and evening availability is ideal.

Discuss with your references what they will say about you; if possible, agree on how they will describe your strengths and weaknesses. It would be best if you and each of your references could agree on one or two weaknesses that are relatively unimportant in relation to the position(s) you are seeking.

Promise to try to contact your references when (or ideally before) their name is given to a potential employer (or search firm). This policy is not only courteous to your references but also helpful to your cause: It gives you the chance to prep references for the specific position for which you are applying.

CREATING A REFERENCE LIST

Develop a standard *reference list.* This page should include each reference's name, title, and organization (if the person is working); address(es) and phone number(s) (office and/or home); a short description of the person's relationship to you (a line or two is fine); and any special notes for the reference checker (to contact the person only at home, at night, and so on). Inclusion of the reference's e-mail address depends on the kind of job you are looking for. Reference checking by e-mail might be appropriate in the high-tech industry, for instance, but generally this would not seem to be the best way to have people contacted.

You can also create a customized *reference list with similar information on a subset of your reference pool for any job possibility nearing the offer stage.* Select those references you think best suited to represent you for the position under consideration.

Bring your reference list to interviews, or be prepared to hand deliver, e-mail, or fax it to the requestor within twenty-four hours. At this critical point in the job-search process, waiting more than a day before responding to the request for references could adversely affect your candidacy.

Consider using your résumé header as the letterhead for your reference list (and letters related to your job search). The header includes your name, address, phone number, and e-mail address. This opening will give your written materials a clean, polished look and will also prominently display your phone number (and possibly e-mail address) on every piece of your correspondence.

USING AND RESPECTING REFERENCES

Contact references in advance each time you plan to submit their names. Describe to them the job you are going for and how you have positioned yourself as an ideal candidate. (Again, coaching your references is acceptable: You are not asking them to lie or misrepresent facts, just to present you in the best possible manner.)

Tell your references that they "might" rather than "will" be called. After all, once you give your reference list to a potential employer, you have no control over the actions of that firm's reference checker. Everyone on your list may not be contacted, particularly if the first few people reached provide favorable assessments. And your most accessible references probably will be contacted first.

Follow up with your references a few days later, and again when a decision is made on the position. If they were called, find out what they were asked and how they thought the conversation went. Make sure you tell them whether you were offered the position.

Don't volunteer your references' names; provide them only when asked and if you are a serious candidate. Avoid subjecting your references to frivolous checks or annoying calls from recruiters or others. If references are requested on an application form, either write, "References will be provided once mutual interest is established," or list them (or attach your reference list) with a note that you should be contacted before they are called. Indicate that, out of courtesy to your references, you have promised to notify them each time they are to be called (which is true).

Contact your references as soon as possible after accepting a new position or rejecting an offer. Thank them profusely for their help and support and, if you turned down an offer, explain why, so that they will remain ready and willing to help when your next job opportunity arises.

3

Résumés

I T WOULD BE NICE to believe that, in your job search, you won't need a résumé, just a hiring manager who will look you in the eye and see the solution to all, or at least some, of his or her problems. But then if that were the case, this chapter would not be the book's longest and most detailed.

The truth is, a good résumé is generally a necessity. Think back to what I said in the Introduction about the job search being both an intellectual and emotional process. Producing a good résumé is an important emotional step for most job seekers. It indicates that you are ready to get moving in the search process.

A résumé is two very different things. It is primarily a *tool* intended to help you secure interviews. It outlines your skills, education, experience, and accomplishments; it highlights your key selling points; and it indicates how you can solve a potential employer's problems. But it is also a *process* whereby you review your background in detail, identifying your primary tasks and responsibilities, the skills you used, the knowledge you acquired, and the results you achieved. Going through this process will help you create the tool and, almost more important, will prepare you for interviewing.

Unfortunately, a résumé often acts primarily as a screening device—résumé reviewers often use it more to eliminate candidates than to choose them. You can do little about this job-search reality other than to emphasize networking and to avoid always leading with your résumé in the search process.

RÉSUMÉ PREWORK

Recognize, and be ready to articulate and document, your knowledge, skills, and experience. Communicate these aspects clearly in your résumé and as you speak with potential employers, agencies and search firms, network contacts, and to anyone else who will listen.

Determine, document, and quantify your accomplishments. Review every previous job and assignment for your tasks and responsibilities, the skills you used, and where and how you had an impact, no matter how small. Areas in which you had an impact constitute your *accomplishments*, which illustrate your potential for solving problems and taking advantage of opportunities; thus they are the best evidence of your knowledge, skills, and experience in action. Think of things you are proud of, things that you made (or helped to make) happen, either individually or as a team member, regardless of whether these achievements were formally recognized by the organization. These are your accomplishments.

A useful exercise in uncovering accomplishments is to develop "PAR" statements or stories, whereby *P* = the *P*roblem, situation, or task that was addressed; *A* = the *A*ction(s) taken, either individually or as part of a team; and *R* = the *R*esult(s), ideally one(s) that can be quantified. PAR statements are essentially short stories describing key things you've accomplished in a work or other setting. This is the material that you restate as bulleted points in your résumé, but it is also what you tell interviewers. In response to an interviewer's question, for example, you might say, "Yes, I've done that three or four times. Let me give you an example. We uncovered the following *Problem*. . . . I led a team of five that took the following *Actions*. . . . As a *Result*, production for that period doubled. Would you like more information on that situation, or would you like another example?" I've seen these called "STAR" statements: *S*ituation, *T*ask, *A*ction, and *R*esult. You also might add a lowercase "s" for skills (PAR*s* or STAR*s*) to consider more consciously the skills you used in these activities.

Any written performance appraisals you have are an excellent source for accomplishments, but you should not depend on them solely. Focused discussions with current or former managers, co-workers, any direct reports, and even customers, clients, and suppliers may uncover accomplishments you have forgotten or perhaps undervalued.

Job seekers often find it difficult to compose accomplishment statements because they are not used to thinking and writing about themselves in sales and marketing terms. The time you spend identifying, clarifying, articulating, and *quantifying* your accomplishments, however, will be well worth the effort. For help with identifying accomplishments, consult Richard Bolles's previously mentioned *What Color Is Your Parachute?*, Martin Yate's *Knock 'Em Dead*, Kenneth and Sheryl Dawson's *Job Search: The Total System*, similar job-search books, and outplacement manuals (the latter if you are out of work and using an outplacement service).

Recent graduates with limited or no full-time work experience should emphasize educational background, skills, and academic, social, athletic, and other accomplishments in their résumés. You are primarily selling your potential, along with your youthful enthusiasm.

The focus on accomplishments, particularly for job seekers with work experience, is a key change in résumés, and in the overall job-search process, that has occurred during the past ten to fifteen years. The concept of accomplishments has been promoted by career and job-search counselors for even longer, but most current job seekers now identify, articulate, and emphasize them.

Make sure you develop numerical values for the accomplishments you cite in your résumé, expressing them in numbers, dollars, or percentages. Quantifying your accomplishments is the best way to demonstrate the impact you had in previous jobs or assignments. The numbers will attract employers' (and search firms') interest by adding believability, punch, and excitement to what might otherwise be somewhat boring résumé prose. Present the numerical values of your accomplishments in the way that will make the strongest statement but also try to use a variety of approaches; for instance, one time you might express the values in percentages and another in actual numbers.

An outplacement candidate of mine, a former IBM business analyst, had an accomplishment bullet on his draft résumé that stated, "Re-engineered [a certain] business process and eliminated a headcount of one." When I asked what the prior headcount had been, he said. "Two." I suggested that he change the text to "Eliminated headcount by 50%." This rephrasing makes the same point, and honestly, but with much greater impact—the job search *is* a marketing and sales process.

CREATING A RÉSUMÉ

Write your own résumé. The process of creating a résumé will help you prepare for the overall job-search process. Completing a document that you have worked hard on and are proud of will significantly boost your confidence about finding your next job. It is an important step in the intellectually and emotionally challenging job-search process.

Having someone else write your résumé poses several problems. The writing style of your prepared résumé is likely to differ from that of the accompanying cover letter you compose, and this difference may not go unnoticed. In addition, it is likely that interviewers will sense quickly that the résumé's language does not match your conversational style.

Although you should write your own résumé, seek feedback from as many others as you would like (or can stand). But remember that it is *your* résumé, not theirs. You don't have to make changes to accommodate every comment you receive, and you should never make the excuse when someone challenges something on your résumé that "so and so suggested I put it that way." Deciding what stays and what goes is *your* responsibility.

Have a single résumé, if possible, to support your job-search efforts. Logistically, it will be much easier for you. If, however, you determine that you need multiple versions of your résumé targeted at specific areas, that's fine, but be sure that each version is unique and carefully tailored for its area of focus.

Some very organized and detail-oriented job seekers (and probably ones with excellent computer resources available to them) create a new version of their résumé for every opportunity they go after. But do you want to do that? Besides having to undertake the extra work involved, are you sure you will guess right for each résumé change you make? You might take out the wrong item, or add something that a résumé reviewer will not like. Rather than spend extensive time and effort on tailoring résumés, create a single "good enough" résumé, then concentrate on the more difficult aspects of the job search, particularly networking. (The concept of a "good enough" résumé is explained in the "Finalizing a Résumé" section at the end of this chapter.)

Start by developing a résumé in the standard reverse-chronological format. The discipline required in reviewing all your past jobs and assignments to create a reverse-chronological résumé not only will help prepare you for interviews but may uncover forgotten tasks, responsibilities, and accomplishments. A reverse-chronological résumé also will provide most of the raw material you will need if you later decide to switch to a functional or a combination format. (These alternate approaches are discussed in the "Other Résumé Versions" section.)

Even for experienced people determined to make a career change, it's best to begin by drafting a résumé geared toward your current or most recently held position. This initial version then can be put on the shelf while you pursue a new career direction and work on a version of your résumé geared toward that change. The on-the-shelf version will be available if the career change proves improbable, or impossible, for any reason.

Keep your résumé simple and straightforward. Include the following (and generally in this order):

- your name, address, and telephone number(s), labeled appropriately if there is more than one number.

- your e-mail address if you have one and can be reliably contacted that way.

- your job objective (this section is optional; it is discussed in "The Major Sections" later in this chapter).

- a summary of your experience, knowledge, and skills.

- your experience/work history that cites organization(s), job title(s), location(s), and begin and end dates (in this section, you should describe tasks and responsibilities but emphasize accomplishments).

- your formal education and professional training.

- other potentially relevant information (this material is also optional), such as certifications, publications, patents, awards, foreign-language proficiency, professional and community affiliations, and so forth.

Recent graduates normally put education before experience. They also can get away with omitting an objective or a summary because what they primarily are selling is their potential, not their specific experience. If they do have a clear focus area, however, including an objective might strengthen their case.

Provide only enough information to interest the reviewer in inviting you in to interview. Avoid "overstuffing" your résumé; save some material for face-to-face discussions.

Limit your résumé to two pages or less. Anyone can use a one-page résumé, and some job seekers feel strongly about keeping theirs to one page, which is fine. But most experienced people go with two pages. (More than 95 percent of the thousands of experienced people I've worked with over the past decade have opted for a two-page résumé.)

Potential employers might view a résumé that is more than two pages as sign of your laxity—that you haven't put in the work required to consolidate the material into two pages. Of course, if the person who reviews your résumé has a three- or four-page résumé, he or she may not mind, but such individuals are in the minority.

If you use a two-page résumé, put the most important information on the first page (except for the specifics of your education and any professional training, which reviewers usually expect to see at or near the bottom of the second page). Put your name and "Page Two" on the second page, typically at the top, so that, if separated after being received, the pages stand a chance of being reunited. Don't, however, include your full résumé header (name, address, phone number, and e-mail address) on the second page, because a reviewer glancing at the header could easily mistake your second page for a complete one-page résumé. Some job seekers omit their address on the page two header but include their phone number (or e-mail address) along with their name. This is fine as long as the header is easily distinguishable from the page one header.

Try to balance the text across the two pages. Include white space between the text blocks to stretch out the material to a full two pages rather than cramming the material into a page and a half. Keeping the most significant information on the first page, however, is more important than precisely balancing the text.

Avoid stapling a two-page résumé: Often the first thing a recipient does upon receiving a résumé is to separate and photocopy the pages, and you cannot count on anyone being gentle or taking the time to use a staple remover.

Rather than exceed the two-page limit, provide additional information (for instance, extensive lists of company-sponsored training, publications or patents, professional affiliations, relevant community activities) on one or more separate addendum pages that can be used when appropriate, but not every time you submit your résumé. An addendum page should begin with your full résumé header followed by "Résumé Addendum" and a line labeling what it is (for example, "Publications" or "Professional and Community Affiliations"). This way, the recipient will immediately understand that this addendum page is not part of your basic, no-more-than-two-page résumé.

If you are a recent college graduate with little experience besides summer jobs and internships, keep your résumé to one page. A two-page résumé from someone who has just completed an undergraduate program might be viewed as indicative of an overactive ego: You don't have that much experience yet.

Don't make your résumé too dense. You can keep a wordy résumé down to one or two pages by decreasing the margins and eliminating nearly all the white space or by having adequate margins but adjusting fonts, point size, and line spacing to get a lot of words into your text blocks. If you make your résumé too hard to read, however, it probably will not be read, or else it will leave the reviewer with a negative impression.

Write your résumé in terms of hiring organizations' needs. I don't mean a specific organization here, although that sometimes may be the case. Rather, I am suggesting that you craft your résumé from the viewpoint of hiring organizations and hiring managers. The résumé reviewer is primarily concerned with finding a candidate whose skills, knowledge, and experience match the employer's interests and needs. Make sure your résumé is constructed to clearly and powerfully answer these questions: "Why should we consider this person [you] for our organization and open position?" and "How will he or she help us solve our problems?"

Avoid the common mistake of having your résumé read like a job description. Many résumés simply list duties and responsibilities rather than also stating and emphasizing accomplishments. The former approach fails to explain how you added value to a current or previous firm, or how you would add value to a potential firm if hired. Employers want someone who will have a positive impact on their organization. Your previous accomplishments are the best evidence that you can and will do that if hired.

Some job seekers rely too much on the text of the job description for their current job or previous ones in preparing their résumé. A tip-off for résumé reviewers is inclusion of phrases such as "as required" or "as needed."

Omit any negative aspects of your work history, education, skills, and personal life, and eliminate items that usually are irrelevant and might even disqualify you. Because the job search is a marketing and sales process, you want to emphasize the positive and downplay the negative in your résumé and other job-search material. Also, omit information that is not relevant to your potential work performance and that might be harmful to your candidacy: age, height and weight, health, marital or family status, reasons for leaving previous positions, and religious or political affiliations.

Omission of personal information from an experienced job seeker's résumé is another significant change that has occurred in the job-search process during the past ten to fifteen years. Recent graduates often include this information, however, to give the résumé screener or hiring manager a glimpse of their personality and interests, to provide possible items for making connections with résumé reviewers and interviewers, and for the small talk that normally occurs at the start of an interview.

Be honest in your résumé; present yourself accurately, but focus on the positive. Don't in any way misrepresent yourself or your skills, knowledge, experience, accomplishments, or education, but always be ready with a positive presentation of anything from your past that could be perceived as a negative. View your résumé and other efforts at marketing yourself in terms of emphasis and appropriate omission.

Include important points in your résumé rather than saving them for your cover letter. Because cover letters are not always read, or are not always read first, significant items may be missed.

Remember that anything you put on your résumé might become a topic of conversation in an interview. If you are a wine aficionado, for instance, cite this hobby on your résumé only if you are prepared to, and wish to, discuss it. And, though some résumé reviewers may appreciate (while others will ignore) a reference to your hobby, the inclusion may alienate a teetotaler. Again, anything you do in the job search will appeal to some people and dissuade others.

Never date your résumé. Some people put the month and year (or the actual day) they produced the version at the end of their résumé. Doing so adds no value to your résumé and, after time passes, makes the résumé look dated.

THE MAJOR SECTIONS

A standard reverse-chronological résumé has four or five major sections, although other sections can be added as appropriate (or this additional information can be provided in a résumé addendum).

- The *header* has your name and detailed contact information.

- An *objective* and/or a *summary* is provided to help the résumé reviewer get an overall sense of who you are, what you are looking for, and what you can offer the organization.

- The *experience* section highlights where you've worked, for what time period, what your role is or was, and what was accomplished in each position.

- Your formal education and any applicable training are provided in an *education* or *education and training* section.

- A section labeled *other* (or more specifically titled) can be included at the end of a résumé.

Header

Start with a header containing your name and contact information—address, phone number(s), and e-mail address. Label phone numbers appropriately, but only if there is more than one number. Use an e-mail address only if e-mail is a reliable way to contact you. There is no need to label the sheet "Résumé" or "Résumé of . . . "; this is obvious.

Most often the name and contact information are stacked and centered at the top of the first page, but there is no rule that says they must be formatted this way. The header can be the one place to make your résumé a bit more distinctive—and remember that the header you create can become the letterhead for your job-search letters and reference list. This area of the résumé is also a place to save a little space by using a design other than the semi-standard, stacked and centered, one-item-per-line format.

Though multiple telephone numbers should be clearly labeled, if you provide only one number, you don't have to preface it with "Phone" or "Tel." (readers know what it is) or indicate "Home" (readers assume it to be either a home number or the best place to reach you). And you don't have to label your e-mail address as such (most readers will know what it is).

Some people simply insert a line between the header and the rest of the résumé. Others put their name on one side (usually the left), with the contact information on the other, or else center their name but split the contact information between the left- and right-hand sides. Another approach is to use a line, but to put your name above it and the contact information below it. There are many header variations that, when done tastefully, can make your résumé look a little more distinctive without changing the basic text (and perhaps save a line or two on the first page).

Make sure that your name in the header appears at least as significant as the next most significant element of your résumé. For example, if you style your section headers boldface and in all capital letters, then do the same with your name in the header. Some job seekers increase the point size of their name slightly to make it stand out more. Although it is best to use one font and one point size throughout a résumé, point size variability in this case is generally acceptable. Some people reduce the point size of their contact information to put more emphasis on their name; if you do that, be sure you don't make the contact information too small to be easily read.

Objective and/or Summary

Omit an objective unless you can create one that is clear, focused, value-added, and written in terms of employers' needs. The days of including a résumé objective such as "Seeking [an unspecified] challenging position in a growing company that values its employees" are long past. Even if a challenging position in a growing company is exactly what you want (although it may be a bit unrealistic to expect), don't advertise your goals to potential employers who are only interested in what you can do for them, how you can help them solve their problems. Once an employer has offered you a job, you can complete your analysis to determine if your needs will be met by accepting the position. Also, you can determine if there are aspects of the formal offer that need to be addressed in a negotiation process (see Chapter 10).

A résumé objective can be very appropriate for recent graduates who have a specific focus area (or areas). Recent graduates using an objective, however, should have another, more generic résumé version without an objective in case an interesting opportunity arises outside their primary focus area(s).

***Include a summary section in most cases, particularly if you are not
using an objective.*** You can have both sections, but most job seekers
with prior work experience now use only the former. A summary
statement can be difficult to write, but it is important because the
résumé screener often will glance through it first to determine if your
résumé is worth reading. A summary can be viewed as an implied
objective if you are an experienced person going for a position similar to what you had before, or for a different position but one for
which you are qualified based on your skills, experience, accomplishments, or education.

If you can easily categorize yourself (for example, administrative
professional, consultant, financial analyst, general manager, human
resources vice president, senior marketing specialist, software engi-
neer, training director), include this label in the first line of the summary, or, even better, as the first few words. This wording will help the
screener "slot" you, assuming that you feel comfortable with, and
want to be, "slotted" in your job search.

Though it is common but certainly not mandatory to reference
the total years of experience in a summary, people with extensive
experience often seem determined to specify the exact number of
years of their experience in the summary. Most employers today,
however, are looking for skills and accomplishments rather than
just years of experience. And a person with, say, twenty-seven
years' experience might have just one year's experience twenty-
seven times. If you do have that much experience, you could state
"over 25" years or even "over 20." Both statements are true and
show that you have significant experience, but they don't overemphasize a specific number. Also, you don't have to refer to the specific number of years in the summary; résumé reviewers can
ascertain this information from the employment dates in the experience section.

If you have trouble creating a summary, try completing the rest of
the résumé text first and then summarizing the information in no
more than three to five lines. Including a bulleted list in this section
is also effective.

Recent graduates can omit a summary and start with the education section. The latter will be their main selling point in most cases.

The importance and widespread use of a summary for job seekers
with work experience is another significant change that has occurred
in résumé preparation during the past ten to fifteen years.

If you make general points in your summary, have one or more examples of each point in the résumé body. As with oral presentations, tell your audience what you are going to tell them, then tell them. Here are some examples:

- If you state in your summary that you have "extensive international experience," list in the experience section some of the countries you have worked in or which firms you have worked with; also state what you accomplished in each situation.

- If you indicate in your summary foreign-language proficiency that you have used to advantage in business, make it clear later how and where this proficiency was used.

- If you state "achieved significant cost savings" in your summary, provide specific examples (with numbers) of these savings in the experience section.

- If you claim in your summary that you have "special expertise" in some area, make sure this expertise is clearly demonstrated through the accomplishment statements in the résumé body.

- If you use a functional or a combination résumé format and have labeled subsections in the selected accomplishments section, you might want to include these titles or an equivalent reference in the summary as areas of significant expertise. (Again, tell your audience what you're going to tell them and later give them the specifics.)

Highlight your computer or other technical skills. Because jobs at all levels now require computer skills, noting in your résumé that you have them might put you at an advantage. Other technical skills also can be critically important, depending on your field and the position you are seeking. Many job seekers include this information as part of the summary; others place it in a separate computer skills or technical skills section between the summary and experience sections or near the end of the résumé. Just be sure to include it somewhere.

If your computer skills are minimal, leave this fact out. If your skill levels vary greatly, consider using phrases such as "proficient at," "experienced with," and "trained in" to differentiate your skill levels, unless you would prefer to hide this fact until you have an interview. The strategy can be risky, but in a marketplace that places such a high premium on computer proficiency, it might be necessary to get you in the door. In general, be specific about the software programs you have used if they are current and would add to the overall story you are try-ing to tell.

Experience

Document your work history with employer names, locations, dates, and job titles. Including just the years is usually sufficient (rather than indicating both months and years), unless you have only a few months or years of full-time experience. For locations, use city/town and state, or country if outside the United States.

One way to account for obvious gaps in your work history is to address them explicitly in the experience section. You might adapt wording from the following examples:

In school full time	**1990–1992**
At home with child	**1985–1988**

In any case, be prepared to answer questions about gaps. Résumé reviewers commonly pride themselves on being accomplished "gap hunters." Employment gaps of less than a year or two can be hidden by citing only years and not months in your work experience.

Recent graduates or those out of college just a year or two some-times use months and years.

Show the overall time you worked for each employer, plus the time you spent in each job if you had multiple positions. If you held mul-tiple jobs for one employer, use formatting to clearly distinguish between the overall and specific dates. For example, put the overall time with the organization in boldface type and the time spent in each position in nonboldface type, or put the overall time on the right-hand or left-hand side, with the time spent in each position fol-lowing the related job title. There are many ways to distinguish between your overall time with the firm and the time you spent in specific jobs/assignments; choose one that will be immediately obvi-ous to anyone reviewing your résumé.

You might choose not to include the overall years with an orga-nization if you worked many years for one employer and perhaps only for that employer. In that situation, you might eliminate the overall dates with that single employer to downplay the fact that you spent so much time at one firm. You are not being dishonest, as the dates provided for specific jobs/assignments will show exactly how long you worked at that organization.

Consider including brief descriptions of the organizations for which you have worked. You might want to note size, sales volume, products, competitive position, relationship to another (for example, a parent) firm, and so on. These descriptions can be particularly important if the firms for which you have worked are not well known. Customarily, this information about the organization is provided directly beneath the organization name in the experience section, and it often appears in *italics* to differentiate it from what you did. If space on your résumé gets tight, however, these brief descriptions are one of the first things to consider deleting, as they usually contribute much less than, say, a bulleted list describing your personal accomplishments.

Emphasize your pertinent career accomplishments in terms of the problems or challenges you faced, the actions you took, and the business results that were achieved. Accomplishment statements should start with an action verb; should be limited to two to three lines, ideally in one sentence for continuity and varied in the order in which the parts are presented; and should include a quantified result (for instance, a dollar amount, a percentage, or time saved).

Allow the most space for the jobs, responsibilities, and accomplishments that are most relevant to the position you are seeking. Gear your résumé toward the job you are going after. Also, if you are an experienced manager but never want to manage people again, then certainly mention but downplay your managerial skills.

Use active and nonrepetitive language throughout the experience section. Here are some tips to follow:

- Start each sentence or bulleted phrase with an action verb.

- Avoid the phrases "responsible for" and "had responsibility for." Change "Responsible for managing . . . " to "Managed . . ." Be specific wherever possible. Use action verbs that describe what you did and what actually was accomplished, not what you were responsible for.

- Vary the action verbs to avoid repetition and keep the reader's interest. People will often inadvertently use the same word or phrase three or more times in three lines of text. A good résumé editor will point out redundancies to you.

If you have many years of experience and think that providing the details of each job will exceed two pages, or possibly result in your being discriminated against because of age, include only the last ten, fifteen, or twenty years or whatever period is most relevant to the position(s) you are seeking. When using this approach, however, you should at least acknowledge your prior work. One way is to include a "Prior to" statement at the end of the experience section. ("Prior to 1980, held positions as X or Y . . . [and/or] in the Z industry.") This approach makes it clear that, although you don't consider your previous experience relevant to what you are currently seeking, you are willing to discuss this experience in interviews.

If you use this approach to hide your age, then leave out graduation or attendance dates in the education section, as they usually will give away your age. If the earliest position listed was your job right out of school, however, and you include in the experience section the year you started working, don't leave out the dates in the education section—this omission might make you appear older than you are.

Education (and Training)

Put your education near the end of your résumé, unless it is the most significant thing you have to sell. For most people with work experience related to what they are going after, the education (or education and training) section should be placed after the experience section.

The date of any degree is usually sufficient, rather than the dates you attended an institution, unless you did not complete the degree; in this case, include attendance dates. And usually just the year of graduation is sufficient, rather than the month and year.

Job seekers with work experience usually exclude high school information if they attended college (in which case a high school diploma is assumed). It would be relevant, however, to cite a program you completed at a technical high school if that program pertains to the position you are seeking. Mentioning that you attended a prestigious secondary school might impress a résumé reviewer. But then it is also possible that a reviewer will be biased against such "prep" schools, seeing them as a symbol of class privilege. Remember that you cannot presume anything about a résumé reviewer.

The amount of supporting information you include in the education section (minor(s), specific courses taken, awards, major class projects or internships completed, participation in sports or other extracurricular activities) should be based on relevance to the position(s) you are seeking. Also, the longer you have been out of school, the less important these specifics probably are. If you are not a recent graduate, don't make résumé reviewers feel that your undergraduate (or a graduate school) experience was the high point of your life— even if it was. Remember that reviewers generally are more interested in your work experience.

Experienced job seekers who consider their educational background a very important factor in their search sometimes reference their degree(s) in the summary (for example, a Harvard M.B.A. and a Tufts B.A.) but leave the date(s) and other details for the education section. And job seekers who completed their degrees while working often add a line such as "Completed degree while working full time." As always, this statement may make a good impression on some and a poor one on others.

Recent graduates usually start their résumés with the education section, as that is the most important thing they have to sell, and they often include the month and year of graduation.

Include company-sponsored or other professional training, but only if it pertains to the position you are going after and would interest potential employers. This aspect can become more important the further you are from the completion of your formal education. In most cases, don't cite every company or professional training course you completed, particularly if the course list is extensive. (A résumé reviewer might think that all you did was take classes.) If you have an extensive course list that you believe is important to your story, include a subset in your résumé or refer to a more complete list provided as a résumé addendum.

Other Sections

Note any special certifications, awards, patents, publications, professional affiliations, foreign-language proficiencies, and so forth, but only if these skills, affiliations, or achievements are relevant to what you are going after. Again, if the list of these special items is long, consider making it a résumé addendum. If an item is both significant and relevant (you are a CPA looking for a finance position, or you are multilingual and seeking an international position), you might note it in your summary.

Omit the statement once found at the end of many résumés: "References will be provided upon request." This line is simply a waste of space: If you are searching for a job, you must supply references when asked. Even more important, never list the names of your references on your résumé. These people are doing you an important favor, and you don't want them to be pestered needlessly.

RÉSUMÉ FORMATTING AND STYLE

Write résumés that potential employers can quickly and easily glance through. Résumé reviewers typically "eyeball" the document rather than read each word. Their initial perusal, whether it takes ten, fifteen, twenty, or thirty seconds, probably will determine your résumé's future. Can reviewers quickly find what they need, or will they have to struggle, possibly causing your resume to end up in their reject pile? Résumé formatting (along with the use of an objective and/or a summary statement) can greatly aid, or hinder, this perusal process.

Try to make your résumé somewhat unique. Be particularly cautious if you are out of work and using the services of an outplacement firm, or have been otherwise required to use a highly structured format (such as that required for current Harvard Business School M.B.A. students). Similarly, avoid résumé-creation software packages that provide a "one style fits all" format. Typing a two-page résumé (or hiring someone to type it for you) is not very difficult.

Although the highly structured one-page résumé format that Harvard Business School students are required to use is very appropriate for the on-campus recruiting process, soon after graduation a less structured two-page format can be adopted. Inserting an objective and/or a summary statement, moving the education section after the experience section, increasing the point size used, and eliminating personal information are the best primary changes to make.

View your résumé as real estate and yourself as the architect and landscape architect. The items you put on the "property" are very important, but how they look (on the page) is important as well. Use your computer's print preview function to see how your résumé looks on the page.

Use short paragraphs—preferably no longer than three to four lines—or, even better, use a bulleted format. Avoid big clumps of text; they are hard to read and even harder for a résumé reviewer to peruse. Use bullets or an equivalent symbol (boxes or diamonds) rather than asterisks (*), o's (o), or dots (·). And perhaps use dashes (—) if you need further lists under a bulleted entry. If your word-processing software does not automatically insert standard bullet spacing, leave two or three character spaces between the bullets (or dashes) and the text.

Leave sufficient white space throughout your résumé, but don't decrease the point size of your font to achieve an uncrowded appearance. The point size becomes even more significant when your résumé is placed in a "to be reviewed" stack. If your point size is noticeably smaller than that of most of the other résumés in the pile, the reviewer may start off with a less-than-positive impression of you. There are many ways to create the appearance of more space in a résumé.

- Leave adequate but not excessive margins. (After getting the résumé text close to the way you want it, experiment by making minor adjustments to the margins. See how various changes affect the overall "look.")

- Go up one or more point sizes. Look at the result; you may not have to eliminate as many words as you think, and your résumé will be more readable. Don't just be concerned with the absolute point size, however, as 12-point text in the font you have chosen can be noticeably different from 12-point text in a different font. Although it is hard to specify one acceptable point size because of the significant variation in font appearance, 12- or 11-point text works best for résumés with most fonts.

- Leave two lines of space between major résumé sections—this is one of the simplest ways to give your résumé a more spacious feeling. Also leave two lines of space between the header and the text (or the first section header) on page one, and between the abbreviated header and the first line of text on page two.

- Leave half-lines or partial lines of space between the entries of a bulleted list or blocks of text. (For example, Microsoft Word lets you define any line as a "paragraph" and the space above or below it as one point, two points, and so on. Eight to ten points is roughly equivalent to a full blank line.)

- Leave two spaces after periods and colons to aid readability. (Early word-processing programs provided this spacing automatically.) Even minor details, such as the use of two spaces rather than one in this situation, can contribute to the feeling of spaciousness in a résumé.

- Eliminate space-wasting "widowed" words (single words on the last line of a bulleted entry or paragraph). If there is just one word on the last line, rewrite the text to get it down to one less line, thus creating space for more text somewhere else on the page or, even better, leaving more white space. A nonpreferable though acceptable alternative to eliminate the "widow" is adding a word or two to the bulleted entry or paragraph. You also could change the left or right margins, but that change might eliminate the original widow while generating new widows on other lines.

- If you put your dates on the left, try stacking them as shown below, and then moving the text margin to the left a few spaces:

1994–
1996

instead of

1994–1996

- Consider omitting the section header for the summary section. (Because this section, if used, is near the top of the résumé, right after your name and contact information, eliminating the section header will not confuse the reviewer but will save at least a few lines—assuming that you had this header on its own line.) Similarly, if the experience section is split between résumé pages one and two (a common occurrence), there is no need to put "Experience (cont.)" or "[company name] (cont.)" between the page two header and the text. Doing so only wastes space.

Be aware that if you have to fax your résumé—which is almost a necessity these days—the received copy may have been shrunk by approximately 5 percent by the transmitting machine to make room for a fax header. Barely readable text can become unreadable after being received by fax, so make sure that you start off with an adequately large point size.

Use the third person rather than first in résumés. Save "I," "my," "our," and so on for your cover letters.

Limit your use of adjectives such as "successful" or adverbs such as "successfully" to describe things you have done. Provide specific results instead in an accomplishment statement that describes how and why the item was a success.

Use a consistent format and style throughout your résumé.

- Make the format and style of your résumé's section headers consistent: left-justified or centered; all caps, initial caps only, or all lowercase; and so on.

- For the résumé text, use either left justification or left and right justification. If you choose the latter, the word-processing program probably will do some type of proportional spacing, so beware of extra spaces that *you* may have inadvertently added, or lines with large spacing gaps because of the proportional spacing that has been applied. Correct any large spacing gaps by rewording, or perhaps by using a hyphen to bring up part of the first word from the next line. One acceptable exception to the use of consistent justification throughout is to make the summary left- and right-justified and the résumé text left-justified.

- If you use periods at the end of bulleted items, end every bullet with a period.

- In lists of three or more items, either use a comma before the *and* in each list or omit that comma. Whichever choice you make, be consistent.

- If you use *to* between dates ("1990 to 1995"), use it with all dates. If you use dashes instead ("1990–1995"), use them throughout. If you leave a space before and after the dash, do it everywhere or leave out the spaces everywhere.

- Most U.S. job seekers use the postal designation for states (for instance, *MA* for Massachusetts and *NY* for New York), which can save a little space. If you use the postal designation in the résumé header, make sure you use it throughout, or else spell out the state name(s) everywhere. Note that postal designations are not abbreviations so do not require a period.

- Avoid using a variety of fonts or point sizes, or overusing italics, boldface, underlining, and so forth. Be conservative in your use of these styling features, and be aware of the potential problems they can create in résumés that are electronically scanned by the receiving organization.

- Don't use too much capitalization. Some résumé writers use capital letters for emphasis, but too many caps (particularly in the summary) make the text more difficult to read.

- A résumé convention, though not a rule, is to spell out one-digit numbers (except for those that follow a dollar sign or precede a percent symbol) and to use numerals for two-digit numbers and above.

- If you choose to abbreviate *billion* to *B*, *million* to *M* (there is no need to use *MM*), and *thousand* to *K*, do so consistently. These stylistic conventions will also save space.

Will these or similar consistency suggestions guarantee that your résumé will be read, or read carefully? Of course not. Remember—"it depends" is the answer to almost all job-search questions, and that is particularly true regarding résumés. Still, being consistent in your résumé sets a businesslike tone and minimizes items to which the reviewer/screener might react negatively.

Be a ruthless editor, or solicit comments from someone who is. Make every word count. Also realize that résumés are written in stylized language that doesn't necessarily follow the rules of English grammar. If you've nearly finalized your résumé draft and need or want more white space, consider deleting all the definite and indefinite articles (*a*, *an*, and *the*). Read a phrase aloud, and if it sounds okay without certain articles and adjectives (as it will most of the time), leave them out.

FINALIZING A RÉSUMÉ

Give it one last look over, concentrating primarily on the text's appearance. Consider increasing the point size (if you have not done so already), changing the margins, and adding full or partial lines between bulleted items or other bodies of text. Do everything you can to give the reader a greater feeling of space, which will make the résumé easier to read or scan.

Get a number of perspectives on the final, or near final, draft. Seek feedback from a variety of sources, including your references, career counselors or outplacement consultants, search professionals, past managers or supervisors, co-workers, direct reports, academic contacts, and anyone else whose opinion you value. Remember, however, that ten reviewers might give you ten different sets of comments, with some of them diametrically opposed.

Widespread review, particularly by people you have worked for and with, can help uncover forgotten tasks and additional accomplishments. Ask those familiar with your work if you have omitted, overlooked, or underemphasized any accomplishments.

Search professionals have very strong opinions about résumés, and many of their beliefs are valid, as these people are daily brokers in the job-search marketplace. Still, they can have strong biases. Also, if they decide for whatever reason that they won't represent you to their client company or companies, it is unlikely that they will provide free résumé advice unless you can take advantage of some strong connection you have with them (for instance, shared alumni status).

You don't have to make changes to accommodate every comment made about your résumé: You are the one who must be satisfied.

Make sure there are no grammatical errors, misspellings, or typos. If your word-processing program does not automatically check spelling but has a spell-check feature, use it before printing each new version of your résumé. Have others proofread your final version or review it yourself slowly and carefully; reading backward (from the last word to the first) is a good technique.

Automatic grammar-checkers are not too useful in résumé preparation because of the stilted language and lack of complete sentences characteristic of résumés. In addition, the spell-check feature will not distinguish between words such as *their*, *there*, and *they're*, so be sure you have used the correct form of the word.

As part of a final check, ensure that the dates in your experience section are accurate. It is very easy for an error to creep in here that you would overlook but that could confuse (and might concern) a résumé reviewer.

Print your résumé on quality bond paper using a laser printer or a good ink-jet printer; alternatively, get a very clean version made on a good photocopier. Laser printing is preferable. In the past, some job seekers had their résumés typeset, but today's printers and copiers are so good that typesetting is an unnecessary expense, and it limits the flexibility to change your résumé. The stationery you choose can be white, off-white, ivory, light gray, or even light "business" blue.

After printing your résumé on whatever bond paper you choose for your final version, get this original photocopied, ideally on a few different machines. Most of an organization's reviewers will see not your original résumé but a photocopy (perhaps of poor quality), so it is wise to test how the document will look photocopied before you send it out. If you see a problem with the look of any of these copies, change the paper, the margins, the font, or the printer you use for this final version. Then repeat the copy check just described.

Finish your résumé, then move on. There is no such thing as a "perfect" résumé. You want one "good enough" to help get you interviews. Work hard on this document until you achieve a version you are proud of; then turn your energy toward the more difficult aspects of the job search, such as networking, which is how most people find jobs, particularly at senior levels.

Certainly modify your résumé as you go through the search process if you find better ways to state things or identify significant additional accomplishments, but don't think any résumé change will be the key in your job search. Many job seekers make subtle, but what they consider to be important, changes to their résumé, only to have most reviewers completely miss the subtlety.

OTHER RÉSUMÉ VERSIONS

If you choose not to use the standard reverse-chronological résumé, you will want to consider using the primary alternative formats—functional and combination résumés. No matter what format you use, you will need to be aware of special considerations for résumés that will be scanned in or sent via e-mail.

Functional and Combination Résumés

Determine if you need multiple versions of your résumé because of the divergent focus areas of your search. If so, besides modifying the text appropriately, also consider using a different résumé header for the different versions, so you can easily keep them straight.

Consider whether a functional or a combination format might be more appropriate for you. But consider these alternate formats only after completing a good final draft using the more standard reverse-chronological approach. If the reverse-chronological version does the job, stick with it. Most hiring managers and search professionals prefer to see an experienced candidate's background displayed in that format, believing it provides the truest picture of the applicant.

Here are some valid reasons to use a functional or a combination format.

- If you are entering the full-time workforce for the first time or are re-entering after an extended absence.

- If you are changing careers or industries.

- If you have varied, unconnected work experiences.

- If you simply wish to emphasize skill areas rather than specific work history.

Be aware, however, that résumé reviewers (particularly those from agencies and search firms) looking at a functional résumé from an experienced person will commonly ask, "What is this person trying to hide?"

In a *functional résumé*, an accomplishments (or selected accomplishments) section normally comes just after the objective or summary. Unless it contains only a few bulleted entries, divide this section into labeled subsections to help the résumé reviewer, perhaps after introducing the major sections in the summary. A long list of undifferentiated accomplishments can seem disjointed and can be difficult to comprehend. Also include an experience section with employer names and your job title(s), location(s), and dates in the standard reverse-chronological order.

A *combination résumé*, like a functional one, has an accomplishments (or selected accomplishments) section just after the objective or summary, but it also provides some information under specific job titles in the experience section (as there would be in a reverse-chronological version).

Scanned Résumés

When your résumé is finalized in whatever format you decide to use, create a second version that can be scanned. Résumé review at most organizations is still a manual process, but more companies and agencies are installing résumé scanning/database retrieval systems. The following will help you prepare for that scenario:

- Use white paper for the version to be scanned. A potential employer or agency must receive a clean résumé so that its scanner can get a clear image.

- Pick a common font such as Helvetica, Palatino, Times, or New York in a point size ranging from 10 to 14. Use a normal, not a condensed, version of the font.

- Some scanning systems have difficulty with boldface, underscored, italicized, and other styles of type, so you might want to eliminate or at least minimize the use of such features.

- Increase your use of key words. Consider adding at the front a key words section that lists all the nouns and phrases that the scanner should pick up. (You can also include this section as an addendum page.)

- Don't use bullets, lines, boxes, or other graphics.

- Avoid staples; scanners may misinterpret them.

- If you know your résumé will be scanned, use an oversized envelope so that you don't have to fold the résumé; any lines on the folds might be lost in the scanning.

Scannable versions of your résumé may allow you to ignore the "no-more-than-two-pages" rule. A scanner does not care how long your résumé is.

If you are not sure if a company electronically scans the résumés it receives, call and ask. If so, ask if the system has any specific quirks that you should be aware of.

E-mailed Résumés

The technology and techniques used in on-line job searching are changing so rapidly that the following observations may be out of date as you read this.

Develop yet another electronic version of your résumé if you plan to e-mail it. The primary rule is to avoid using special formatting or special symbols. (Use only items that appear on a standard computer keyboard; for instance, asterisks rather than bullets.) Also, eliminate tabs and soft returns wherever possible. In addition, keep in mind the following pointers:

- Save the text as an ASCII file (no character or paragraph formatting).

- It may be better to include the résumé in the e-mailed message text rather than provide it as an attachment. The conversion of an e-mailed attachment at the receiving end sometimes yields strange results. (Until my desktop word-processing program was recently upgraded, I often received résumés e-mailed as attachments and opened them to find thirty- to fifty-plus-page documents containing two to eight pages of gibberish, two or more pages of unformatted résumé, and another twenty to forty pages of gibberish.)

- E-mail a version of your résumé to yourself or others to see what it looks like when received. But remember that just because one recipient receives it without glitches, that is no guarantee that everyone will.

- When you e-mail your résumé during the job search, also send an identical hard copy with an appropriate cover letter through the mail.

4

Preparing Effective Job-Search Letters

OVER LETTER IS THE TERM most often used to describe the letter that accompanies a résumé in job-search mailings. Some job seekers, aware that cover letters are not always read, question the importance of such letters. Others, however, overemphasize their significance, thinking that only in the letter can they convey a key point that will make the difference in their bid for a job. The truth lies someone in between, but because you don't know what will happen when an organization, a hiring manager, or a potential network contact receives your letter, you need to write an effective one.

Prepare a unique cover letter each time you mail, fax, e-mail, or hand deliver your résumé. Include a letter when answering classified ads or responding to other paper or on-line job postings; when forwarding materials to someone who has requested a résumé, or with whom you have scheduled a field research meeting (informational interview); when trying to encourage the creation of a position at a potential employer through direct mail; or when approaching a potential network contact by letter. Avoid taking the easy way out by sending a résumé without an accompanying letter: Cutting corners can undermine your search effort.

If you fax or e-mail a letter and résumé, also send them by mail that same day, so that the recipient will receive a reminder from you (on your good stationery) a few days later. Although it is faster and easier to fax or e-mail a résumé without a cover letter—and may be acceptable in some situations (if the receiver has requested, or is expecting, the fax or e-mail)—including a good, tailored letter can strengthen your argument and show you are serious about the opportunity.

Print or type your cover letter on the same bond paper you used for your résumé, and use a matching envelope. In sending your résumé, you are making a statement about yourself as a businessperson, so look the part. Although getting overly concerned with your competitors in the job search is not helpful, you have to assume that these individuals will be using this approach as well.

Consider using your résumé header as the letterhead for your letters. As with your reference list, this approach will help give your job-search material a clean and polished look. It also guarantees that your contact information is prominently displayed on every letter you send. You don't want to frustrate the recipient of one of your letters who wishes to follow up with you immediately but cannot because you have not made your phone number or e-mail address readily available.

Keep your job-search letters to one page or less. Be thorough but brief, and use your best business-writing skills. Potential employers who are concerned about these skills, and who realize that résumés are written in somewhat stilted language, often look to the cover letter for a better indication of your writing ability.

FOR EACH LETTER

A job-search letter, particularly one responding to an ad or other job listing, should have three major sections of about a paragraph each. In the first section you identify the position you are interested in and how and where you found out about it. Be explicit, as this information may be useful to the listing firm. In the second section you highlight your skills, knowledge, experience, and accomplishments and describe how they meet the requirements of the position as you understand them. (This is the most important section, so you might want to write more than one paragraph.) In the third section you indicate how, where, and when you can be contacted for an interview, and that you will follow up to determine the status of your application.

Write each job-search letter in terms of the hiring organization's needs. Avoid making your history the focus of the letter; rather, address how your accomplishments align with the organization's interests. One way to keep your letter focused on the hiring organization is to limit your use of first-person pronouns. Also, rather than dwell on your past experiences, focus on the future, on how the organization can profit from what you have to offer.

Modify and personalize every letter you send. Try to include at least one sentence that speaks specifically to that employer.

Avoid abbreviations, acronyms, and jargon. It is always safer to use language most people will understand. Without being overly simplistic or talking down to the reader, write your letters as if your reader knows very little about the work you do, unless you are absolutely sure that the letter is going directly to someone thoroughly familiar with your job, discipline, industry, and so forth.

Eliminate outdated language. Phrases such as "yours truly," "pursuant to," "in regards to," and "the undersigned" are no longer in common use. Have a good editor review your early letters to suggest alternatives to these and similarly dated phrases. Stick with "Sincerely" for the closing.

Include this sentence near the end of most job-search letters: "If I haven't heard from you in a few weeks [you define the appropriate time], I will contact you during the week of [cite month and a range of days] to [determine the status of my application, see if you have any additional ideas for me, and so on]." This sentence is included for two reasons: (1) It notifies the recipient that you will call to follow up, and, more important, (2) It gives you a job-search "to do" item for the near future.

Don't say you will call on a specific day, because something might come up to interfere with your ability to follow up on that specific day. Although occasionally you may get a negative response when making these follow-up calls, if you have put time and effort into writing a good letter, you want to know what happened at the receiving end. *Make these follow-up calls,* but perhaps relate the reason for the call first, before giving your name, so you can hang up without disclosing your name if you get a negative reaction.

Center each letter vertically on the page. Short, concise letters are ideal, but leave a good top margin so that the text does appear crammed into the top part of the page.

Make sure your letters are error-free. Proofread them and have others proofread them, if necessary, before you fax, mail, e-mail, or hand deliver them. I once received a "got a job" letter from a job seeker whom I had helped. After my name and address, the letter said "Dear Sandy." Who was Sandy? Probably the last person, or perhaps the first person, to receive this word-processed letter. Such an easily made, but very obvious, word-processing error can sabotage any positive impact of your letter.

Remember to sign each letter. This suggestion applies to mailed, not e-mailed, letters, but, if you can find a way to include an electronically produced signature on your e-mailed letters, you might impress the recipient with your technical acumen.

IN GENERAL

Build a collection of reusable paragraphs as you write multiple letters, but tailor each new one to make it unique. It is not unusual to spend thirty to forty-five minutes or more creating and revising a specific job-search letter, even when you start with a set of paragraphs recycled from your previous letters.

Work hard on your job-search letters, but if you consistently *spend more than an hour preparing each one, you are probably overdoing it.* As with a résumé, there is no such thing as a "perfect" cover letter. It is more important to make these letters "good enough," to get them out, and to write more letters (or, even better, to make more phone calls), than to make each letter perfect.

Review any of the wide variety of books on cover letters, particularly ones with example letters. Among the books to consider are

- *175 High-Impact Cover Letters,* by Richard H. Beatty

- *The Perfect Cover Letter,* by Richard H. Beatty

- *National Business Employment Weekly: Cover Letters,* by Taunie Besson

- *200 Letters for Job Hunters,* by William S. Frank

- *Cover Letters That Knock 'Em Dead,* by Martin Yate

Because there are no perfect letters, however, remember that "it depends" when considering any suggestions in these books on cover letters (or in any other job-search books or articles).

Don't be concerned about whether your letters are read. Questions often arise in the job search about how important cover letters are, given that they frequently are not read. (Often recipients will look at the résumé first, then may or may not go back to the cover letter.) The best approach is to assume that your cover letter *will* be read, and read carefully, so present yourself in the best possible manner.

Include a résumé with most job-search letters; occasionally people with extensive work experience might make an exception and send just a letter. Job seekers with concerns about age discrimination or appearing overqualified sometimes consider omitting their résumés. This is another example of the "it depends" concept, however, because this decision might frustrate some recipients who expect to receive, and want to review, a résumé. Sure, a potential employer could contact you and request a résumé after reading your outstanding letter, but will the organization take that extra step or just throw your letter away? As with most aspects of the job search, it probably will depend on that organization's needs, but don't provide an easy excuse to be screened out.

5

Planning and Executing a Search Campaign

T
HEORETICALLY, THE JOB SEARCH is a simple process: finding a hiring manager who likes you, wants you, and can afford to add you to his or her organization. In reality, of course, the search process is complicated, exhausting, usually frustrating, occasionally exhilarating, and highly unsystematic. Because of these factors, your success rate probably will improve greatly if you develop a plan, acquire the basic equipment and tools, and do the background research required before you execute the plan using the tools and techniques at your disposal. This chapter discusses these diverse but critical topics.

THE PLANNING STAGE

Recognize the two different steps in the job search—getting interviews and then getting offers. You must complete the first step to get to the second, but they are distinct, though often overlapping, phases requiring different skills, strategies, and tactics. As the search process progresses, these two steps often must be carried out simultaneously, which can become confusing.

Plan your work, then work your plan. Set a daily and weekly schedule for yourself and stick to them, but build enough flexibility into your schedules to take advantage of unforeseen opportunities.

Include your spouse/significant other/partner, family members, and close friends in your search planning. Recognize that your job search dramatically affects those close to you, and that it is often beneficial to let these important people in your life be part of the solution.

Think of yourself as a salesperson marketing your problem-solving skills. In selling yourself to a potential employer or hiring manager, you are simply doing what any successful company does—defining a market, developing a product or service for that market, and determining the best ways to reach that market. For most job seekers, these self-marketing duties probably will be some of the most difficult they will ever have to master, but the rewards are great.

If you are out of work, treat your job search as a full-time job. The meaning of *full-time* will differ for individual job seekers because of the intellectual and emotional demands of the search process, but remember that your activity level is one of few things under your direct control in the job search. Finding a job is like working a very demanding job, so it is normally beneficial to work hard during the week and then take the weekend off to recharge your batteries.

Determine your barriers to entering the job market and develop strategies for overcoming them. These strategies could include developing reasoned arguments to counter specific employer concerns, or possibly retraining to add missing skills or to upgrade others. Regardless of whether real barriers exist, most job seekers feel there is something, however minor, that makes them less employable than their competition. (I call it their "Achilles' heel" in the job search, or at least what they perceive to be an Achilles' heel.) Work to overcome this feeling, focusing on how you can help the hiring manager solve his or her problems.

Spend time in libraries or bookstores browsing through the many books and articles on the job search. Many books have been published that offer handy tips and strategies (see the Selected Bibliography), but remember that there are no magic bullets in the job search. As always, "it depends" is the only answer to most job-search questions.

Senior-level people in the job search often rave about John Lucht's *The New Rules of Passage at $100,000+: The Insider's Lifetime Guide to Executive Job-Changing and Faster Career Progress.* This book is particularly good in its coverage of search firms, as the author is a search professional. A companion workbook by Lucht is also available: *Executive Job-Changing Workbook.*

Another book very popular with Harvard Business School graduates is the previously mentioned *In Transition,* by Mary Burton and Richard Widemeyer. It was first published ten years ago but remains up to date with its practical, businesslike approaches to the job-search process. I strongly recommend *In Transition,* particularly for those with an M.B.A. or equivalent experience.

A good book for those out of work is Cliff Hakim's *When You Lose Your Job,* a realistic and well-written novel about job loss and the resulting job search with plenty of "how to" ideas. Hakim's second book, *We Are All Self-Employed: The New Social Contract for Working in a Changed World,* deals with the stark reality of today's workplace.

Contact the alumni office or career center of any colleges or universities you attended. Ask about career services available for alumni or any reciprocal services available at other colleges or universities near you or your intended job-search destination.

Find out if any alumni have volunteered to serve as networking contacts for fellow alums. Ask if an alumni directory is published or available on-line. (Many colleges and universities now publish printed directories, which are often updated and reissued every five years. Some high schools even publish alumni directories.) A directory entry could turn a cold call into a warm call, or at least a lukewarm call.

See if a staff person has been designated as the alumni career advisor (or primary contact). More universities and colleges are formalizing this position and function, as both young and older alumni seek more career and job-search assistance. Sometimes the service is provided by the on-campus career center; other times it is part of the alumni office. Try both places.

Create a thirty- to forty-five-second response to the dreaded "Tell me about yourself" question. It is wise to be flexible and to tailor your response to each situation. Highlight your background, strengths, at least one key accomplishment, and the position(s) you are seeking. Try your response out on business associates, friends, and relatives.

Try not to think about competition for a specific job or competition in general. You can do little or nothing about it. Focus on what you can do for an employer—how you can help the organization solve its problems—rather than on the things you imagine that others can provide and you cannot.

BASIC EQUIPMENT AND TOOLS

Use a high-quality answering machine (or subscribe to the phone company's Call Answering feature); record a clear, short, businesslike greeting. The greeting should give your first and last name and/or verify your phone number. Although this suggestion might raise security concerns for some, remember that a caller with a potential job, job lead, or networking referral might not be familiar with your voice but would like to know that he or she called the right place (otherwise the caller might not leave a message). The best approach is to provide your name or phone number in the greeting.

The way your voice sounds in the greeting can also be critical. Ask someone you trust to listen to and critique your greeting.

A key advantage of the Call Answering service over a home answering machine is that an incoming call will go to voice mail if you are talking on the phone (or using your single phone line for connection to the Internet). This way the caller will not get a busy signal. Call Waiting—whereby a beeping sound informs you that you have another call when you are using the phone—is another phone company option to consider. Also offered by the phone company is Ringmate, which provides a separate phone number with a distinctive ring. If you use this separate number in your résumé and in other aspects of your job search, then you will know by the ring that an incoming call is job related. If you are concerned about the additional expense of these special features (perhaps because you are out of work), consider discontinuing them when you land a job.

Establish fax and personal computer access, the latter if you do your own word processing. Even gas stations and convenience stores now provide faxing services, but the per-page charge can be steep. Commercial photo shops may offer faxing at fifty cents to one dollar per page. Numerous software packages also exist for sending faxes from your home computer. If you don't have a computer at home, libraries are one source for them; friends and neighbors are another. You should also consider the religious or civic organizations to which you belong—perhaps you can use their computer equipment after hours. Free fax and computer access may be available at your local unemployment office, or at federally funded job-search centers for dislocated workers.

Have personal business cards printed, particularly if you are out of work. Include your name, address, phone number, e-mail address, and if possible a line or two describing your focus area(s). Some job seekers create a bulleted list, similar to a mini-résumé, on their business cards. If done well, this looks good, but it is easy to go overboard with this approach. Even if it would be easy for you to generate these cards on your personal computer, it is better to have them professionally printed so as to have that polished look of raised lettering.

If you are out of work, and even if you have only recently left your previous job, don't hand out your old business cards with your home or temporary office number handwritten in. Have your own business cards made as soon as possible. Two exceptions might be if you are being allowed to use your old office as a base of operations during your job search, or if you are being allowed to remain on the organization's voice mail system. In these cases, however, make it clear to anyone you contact as part of your search that you are no longer with the organization.

RESEARCH

Job seekers should regard doing their own job-search research as a shortcut. It can provide the competitive edge of targeting organizations (and even specific employees) to contact; it can help you prepare for interviews; and it can provide you with a base of knowledge to aid in evaluating offers and making other job-related decisions.

There are two primary research sources: published items (including information available on the Internet) and people. Conduct your company and industry research using both sources; don't depend on just one. This section focuses primarily on published sources; the networking section in Chapter 6 describes the people side. A good book to review on this topic is *Researching Your Way to a Good Job,* by Karmen N. T. Crowther (but keep in mind that it was published in

1993 and the availability of information on the Internet since then has greatly affected the job-search research process).

Visit one or more town, city, or college libraries at least once a week to do company and industry research. Your local library will have more information relevant to your search than you might think, along with an ever-increasing number of hands-on information technology tools.

Get to know reference librarians, potentially your best friends in the search process. Their job is to help you find the information you need, and they have been asked numerous questions related to careers and the job search, particularly during the economic turbulence since the late 1980s. The phenomenal increase of information available on the Internet and on other electronic media (for example, CD-ROM) has made reference librarians an even more important guide in the search process. And, despite the myth of enforced silence in a library, most reference librarians enjoy talking with patrons and helping them find the information they need.

Use the Yellow Pages and the many other published business directories as job-search guides. The Yellow Pages list virtually every business in a geographical area (few employers have unlisted phone numbers). Also review some of the many other printed business directories. Every library will have a slightly different set of hard- and soft-cover directories and other reference materials in addition to the Yellow Pages; this is why it is wise to visit multiple libraries, even if you eventually choose one as your primary research location.

Look for directories specific to the geographic area(s) that interest you, such as *Doing Business in Boston,* by Jeffrey P. Levine. He has written similar directories for New York City, Chicago, Pittsburgh, Kansas City, and the central Pennsylvania area.

Get access to CD-ROM and on-line tools to do research on companies. These automated search tools—for instance, *Career Search, One Source, Dun's Million-Dollar Directory, ABI Inform,* and *Wall Street Journal Interactive*—may be available in local public libraries, college libraries (particularly business schools), and outplacement firms. And don't forget state unemployment offices and federally funded centers for dislocated workers; many are now providing access to automated tools such as *Career Search.*

Become Internet-literate, focusing on the Net's application to the job search and its research capabilities. The Internet job search is the subject of many seminars and books. The books are good for the basics but are outdated as soon as they are published, as the on-line world changes so fast. Two books worth considering, however, are *Job-Hunting on the Internet,* by Richard Bolles, the author of *What Color Is Your Parachute?,* and *Life Work Transitions.com: Putting Your Spirit Online,* by Deborah L. Knox and Sandra S. Butzel.

More and more jobs are being listed on the Internet, but the medium's greatest value in the job search is still as a research tool. Huge amounts of information are available on-line about employers, industries, and so on. Many companies have a home page that often lists their job openings and provides information on products and services, locations, and many other facts about the firm. Many professional associations now have Web sites that provide information about membership, meetings, and other activities.

Decide what you want to accomplish before logging on to the Internet, and keep track of the time you spend on-line. Bookmark any site you might want to return to at another time.

A word of caution: Beware of spending too much time on-line, performing tasks that are not related to your job search. The on-line world is fascinating, but it can be very time consuming, and the variety and excitement that the Internet offers might divert your focus from job-search activities.

EXECUTION

Job seekers should let the famous Nike marketing slogan "Just Do It!" be their rule. Planning and organizing are great in the job search, but the real value is in the execution.

Getting Out and Doing It

Believe in yourself. Confidence in your ability to succeed in the job search will help convey an image of your overall competence. It takes a lot of inner strength to be successful in the intellectually and emotionally demanding search process, but if you hang tough and work hard, you can do it.

Take an active role in your search. Create opportunities for yourself by

- understanding and clearly articulating your knowledge, skills, experience, and accomplishments;

- determining the needs of potential employers and hiring managers;

- communicating with as many people as possible; and

- being flexible, enthusiastic, and politely persistent.

Become a student of the process. Given current economic predictions, you will be looking for a job again, and probably sooner and more often than you would prefer. Learn and implement effective job-search methods and build/reinforce a personal network to help you now and in the future.

Use your résumé to get your foot in the door and to prepare you for the interviewing process. Those are its primary purposes. Don't expect your résumé to do anything more. You won't get hired because you have a great résumé, but having a "good enough" résumé may win you the chance to tell your story in person. That is your goal.

Take calculated risks in your search, based on what you know and what you believe. Force yourself to take a chance on a network contact, a job that is a bit out of reach, or a call to an all-important contact.

   If you get a referral to a CEO or other senior-level person, don't be intimidated by his or her position. The person might refer you to someone else in the organization—perhaps just to get rid of you—but that is still a powerful referral to obtain, as it is when any manager refers you to one of his or her direct reports or someone lower in the organization.

Determine the needs of hiring organizations and specific hiring managers. Do research on prospective employers and specific companies with the goal of ascertaining their concerns, whether or not they perceive these concerns. Consider your abilities in relation to what these organizations must continue to do well and need to do differently.

Determine how requirements are changing for your ideal job(s). Is your position or function being outsourced? If so, who is providing the product or service? Could these outsourcing firms be employers that you should consider on either a permanent or contract basis?

Develop a mature and pragmatic outlook about the search process to counter the erroneous belief that there is an ideal candidate for every job. Hiring managers often fantasize that there is someone in the current job market who meets or exceeds their criteria. Although their wishes may occasionally come true, are hiring managers with pressing needs prepared to wait, and wait, and wait some more? Develop reasoned and rational (but not desperate) arguments to convince hiring managers that, although you might not be the ideal match for the position, their business may be at greater risk if they wait for their "ideal" hire. You will not win all, or even most, of these arguments, but you only need to win one.

Be prepared to experience some unprecedented indignities. Job-search indignities, which are much more noticeable when you are out of work, include repeated rejections, unreturned phone calls, disdain by some because you are in the job market (although this is much less likely now, with so many people having been affected by unemployment and uncertainty since the late 1980s), criticism of your résumé and employment record, and perhaps even discomfort in social settings.

Successful salespeople face, and overcome, indignities such as these on a daily basis. realizing that they are just part of the job. When searching for a job, you are in sales, whether you like it or not. Don't let the indignities discourage you. As with all job-search–related frustrations, they will be easier to cope with if you have additional possibilities on the horizon. Work hard to keep your job-search pipeline full.

Stay up to date in your field and on current events generally. Faithfully read local newspapers, *The Wall Street Journal, Business Week, Fortune, Forbes, Inc., Fast Company*, local business journals, and the publications (and Internet sites) that are most relevant to your field or industry. It is essential that you keep up with trends and training in your discipline or industry. Hiring managers often expect job seekers to be aware of the latest developments. Staying informed demonstrates that you were not so entrenched in your last (or current) job that you have lost touch with what is happening in your field or industry.

Find out about and use free (or inexpensive) job-search resources in your community (or nearby). You may have to do some digging, but they are out there. Start with local job-search support groups (if they don't exist in your area, consider starting one) and with the job-search component of the state unemployment office, but don't stop there. The number of federally funded, state-run or -sponsored programs on the job search and entrepreneurship for dislocated workers is growing, as is the federal funding available for retraining.

Consider taking an adult education course to sharpen your skills. Besides obtaining information and developing new skills, you will meet new people—yet another networking opportunity.

Don't make it a rule to avoid a potential employer's human resources (HR) department. Although career and outplacement counselors (and often other job seekers) sometimes advise that you steer clear of HR, this clearly is an "it depends" situation. HR departments may be ineffective and viewed poorly in some organizations but highly valued in others. In the latter case, trying to avoid the HR department may hurt your candidacy.

Be polite and persistent in your networking and other search efforts. *Politeness* is necessary because searching for a job is all about doing the things your mother taught you to do (being nice to people, writing appropriate thank-you notes in a timely manner, remembering people's names). You don't want to turn off anyone by being even slightly obnoxious, even though you will at times get frustrated with the job-search process. *Persistence* is required because, despite their declared urgency to fill an open position, filling it will never be as important to the hiring manager and organization as it is to you as an applicant. Normal work issues and other crises often will divert their attention from the hiring process. Similar delays will occur with some promises made to you by network contacts (even when they are good friends or have only the best intentions).

Get in or stay in good physical shape. The job-search process is an intellectually, emotionally, and physically demanding one. Begin or continue with an exercise regimen to help build your stamina and also to provide you with a physical outlet for the emotional frustrations that are inevitable in the search process. Take things out on a punching bag (or by "pounding the pavement") or other physical exertion rather than on your family and friends.

Considering and Implementing Options

Do, or at least consider doing, a parallel search. Although the concept of focus is critical in the job search, putting all your efforts in one limited area may be emotionally devastating if you have little or no success. Identify, develop, and implement parallel or backup goals and strategies, or at least be on the lookout for these possibilities.

"Listen" to your search. What is working and what is not? Do you need to increase your activity level, extend your focus area(s), change directions, or get professional help for job-search concerns or emotional issues?

If you are out of work, consider taking a temporary or contract position. Part-time work is best, as you can more easily continue your job-search efforts. Temporary/contract workers are in demand at all organizational levels. This kind of work can offer significant advantages to people seeking new jobs or new careers, including the following:

- **Flexibility:** Short-term assignments (or contract work of fewer than forty hours per week) might allow you time to schedule interviews and perform other job-search activities. Many managers of temporary and contract workers have become more sensitive to the need for flexibility in regard to the search process (for example, to allow for scheduling interviews).

- **New experiences:** You can gain experience in different companies and industries, add new skills and accomplishments to your résumé, and generate new stories to tell at interviews.

- **Training:** Temp agencies might help you to build your skills in areas such as computer applications.

- **Practice:** Working in a variety of settings gives you the opportunity to develop, hone, and market your transferable skills, while also enlarging your personal network.

- **"Foot in the door"**: Companies often hire for full-time positions from their temporary pools or from contractors/consultants who have demonstrated their value to the organization.

- **Income:** Last but certainly not least, temporary or contract work is a way to bring in money, although it may affect unemployment benefits if you are out of work. Check with your state unemployment office on this aspect.

For those interested in executive- or professional-level temporary assignments, see *The Directory of Temporary Placement Firms for Executives, Managers, and Professionals.* As an indication of the explosion of activity in this area, the 1999 edition of this directory lists more than 1,950 firms; the previous edition, in 1995, listed 225. Two recent books discussing this growing phenomenon are *Executive Temping: A Guide for Professionals,* by Saralee Terry Woods, which includes a twenty-four-page directory of temporary firms, and *Executive Temp,* by Diane Thrailkill.

When using temporary or contract work as a short-term job-search strategy, be realistic and recognize that it is difficult to maintain an active search while adjusting to the intellectual and emotional demands of any new position, even one that is part time. Also, some job seekers who are successful at obtaining one contract assignment after another sometimes find it difficult if they later look for permanent positions. (In some fields you can get pigeonholed as a "contractor.")

Getting and Staying Organized

Be ready at all times. Carry copies of your résumé, your calendar or appointment book (or the electronic equivalent), personal business cards, reference lists, memo paper, lists of target organizations, folders with information on current prospects, and any other information relevant to your job search.

Write letters and work on your job-search "system" primarily at night. You then will be available to make phone calls and perform other networking activities during the day.

Investigate, and strongly consider, using software to help you get (and stay) organized. Although it is possible to organize your search activities with index cards or file folders, computer applications such as ACT, Lotus Organizer, and Microsoft Outlook (or even spreadsheet software) can make the process more efficient and easier to manage. (Just make sure you don't spend too much time playing with these software applications; they should augment and support your search activities, not replace them.)

Maintain and track your search activity level. Your activity level is one of the few things you have control over in the job search. Measure your progress by counting the number of

- job-search-related phone calls you make and e-mail messages you send daily,

- letters you send and networking/field research meetings you have weekly, and

- interviews you have monthly.

Set numeric goals in each category. Regularly review your progress in relation to these goals and, where necessary, adapt your strategies and tactics to achieve them. But remember that, because the job search is an art and not a science, raw statistics will not tell the whole story.

Being Realistic

Focus on the activity, not the final outcome. If you learn the necessary skills and use them often, you are bound to find a job—and optimally the "right" job for you. You need to be consistent and patient, because you cannot control the employment process and hiring decisions that organizations make.

Understand that, in addition to the amount and quality of your search efforts, other factors can affect the length of the process. These factors include:

- Your attitude (particularly if you lost your prior job and/or your search drags on)

- The condition of the job market (in general and in your industry, field, or location in particular)

- The job type and salary level (the higher you go, the fewer opportunities are available)

- Your geographic limitations or preferences

- Factors beyond your control (age or other types of discrimination)

- Timing

- Luck

Attitude and *activity* are perhaps the two most important personal factors in the job search. They also are the primary things that you, as a job seeker, have some control over. Intelligent, focused, consistent, and productive activity can create a more positive attitude. Three other very important personal factors are *accomplishments*, *focus*, and *courage*—the courage to do the hard tasks in the job search, such as making a lot of phone calls to strangers or near strangers.

Don't wait for a "perfect" job for you; it might never come along. Strive for your ideal position(s) but be realistic about what is available given the market conditions, your qualifications, and any limitations such as geographical preferences. Be flexible and open to options. Don't miss an opportunity because you see only one possible alternative.

EFFECTIVE TELEPHONE USE

Effective phone use is often a key aspect of a successful job-search process. It is vital for networking, collecting information (research), following up, and setting up interviews and other meetings. Everyone finds phone use difficult to some degree, but you still need to be effective at it. Many of the following points also apply to, or can be adapted for, e-mail communications.

Make warm calls (ones in which you use a referral name or other connection) whenever possible, or even exclusively. For most job seekers, cold calls are much more difficult to make, and the success rate usually is much lower. A small percentage of job seekers use cold calls well, but most try to get a referral.

Get organized before making calls. Identify what you want from each call. Prepare an interesting opening statement, including a referral if possible. Use a script or a list of bulleted points, and consider taking notes on a paper copy of this information during each call. Anticipate points of resistance and objections; prepare responses to them. Although you don't have to leave a voice mail message, at least be ready to leave one if given the opportunity (or no other option).

When you reach the person you want, use a referral if you have one, and get to the point of your call quickly. Keep your tone warm. Be cordial, positive, and not apologetic. Do not abuse the privilege of immediate contact that the phone provides. The person you call probably will be less patient than he or she would be face to face, and may be involved in something when you call. Ask, "Have I caught you at a bad time?" If so, arrange to call the person back at a specific time, but one of his or her choosing.

Keep in mind the following telephone etiquette tips:

- Take notes during your calls.

- Be conscious of time but avoid sounding rushed.

- Look into a mirror when calling and smile—it makes your voice come across differently.

- Stand up while talking on the phone.

- Be polite and enthusiastic, regardless of what happens.

Deal effectively with secretaries/assistants/screeners. Here are some suggestions:

- Get the person's name early on (or ahead of time from the switchboard), then use it.

- Introduce yourself and spell your name if necessary.

- Have a good response ready for "What is this call in reference to?"

- Try to develop rapport and get the person on your side.

- Treat the person with courtesy and respect.

- Thank the person for his or her assistance.

    Alternatively, try to avoid them by calling before 8 A.M. or after 6 P.M.

Get comfortable with voice mail. When leaving a voice mail message, you at least get to tell your story without interruption. But be sure that both the tone of your voice and the words you choose are good reflections of your positive, can-do attitude. And with voice mail messages, leave your phone number at least twice, ideally at the beginning and then near the end of your message. That way, if one statement of the number gets garbled, there is another to fall back on.

Make any voice mail message you leave creative and interesting enough that the receiver will want to call you back. Sometimes just the strength of the referral or other connection will accomplish this. But never wait too long for a return call. Be persistent, but politely so.

Perhaps consider a policy of not leaving messages on voice mail but instead to keep calling back. This approach gives you a certain amount of control, but it requires that you make a lot more calls.

Check any messages you leave for accuracy. Errors can easily be made when a person takes a message or when one is left on an automated system. Politely ask a message taker to read back the message, particularly the phone number you left. With voice mail, listen to any system directions. Press the indicated key after you are finished recording (if given the option), then listen to any additional options available. If possible, review your message before sending it and rerecord it if you don't like what you said or the way you said it. If given the option of marking a voice mail message "urgent," resist this temptation in most cases.

Vary the type of messages when leaving multiple messages for the same person. Perhaps one time ask for voice mail rather than to be directly connected, and at another time try to get an assistant or someone else to take a message. Sometimes don't leave a message, so it will not appear that you are calling too often and pestering the person you are trying to contact. Again, polite persistence is the key, as it is in most job-search activities.

Batch your outgoing calls. It helps to get some momentum when making job search-related phone calls. If you batch them by time period, or by number of calls, you will probably see better results. And plan to work for an hour or two (or to make fifteen to twenty calls), not just to work five minutes (or to make five calls).

Also realize that if you make twenty calls, you will probably get voice mail fifteen times, reach a person to take a message three times, and actually talk with only two of the people you were calling. These are the odds for today's job seeker.

Develop a strategy for following up on the messages you leave. Again, be polite and persistent.

Don't subject your ego to too much torture: Know when to stop calling for the day. The more warm calls you make, of course, the less emotional damage you are likely to experience. Keep at it until you have placed the number of calls you planned, but, if you reach that number while you are on a roll, keep going until your energy runs out.

Be prepared for telephone interviews, but avoid them if possible. Screeners (often those from the human resources department), search professionals, or even the hiring manager may do initial phone screening, so you may not have a choice. But if you can, try to get face to face for screening interviews.

Try to reschedule if a call from an employer or search firm catches you at a bad time. Say that you are just about to leave for an appointment (it is okay to stretch the truth here) and schedule a specific time for them to call back (or for you to call them).

6

Primary Job-Search
Strategies

EACH OF THE FOUR main job-search strategies—networking, targeting organizations, using agencies and search firms, and responding to classified ads and other job postings—is covered in this chapter. Some people may assert that it is time to identify use of the Internet as a separate major strategy, but I still view it primarily as a job-search tool (although potentially a very powerful one, particularly for researching companies and industries).

Use all the primary strategies when you pursue your next position. Decide how much time and effort to devote to each, but remember that the easiest strategy—just responding to ads, or relying exclusively on search firms or Internet job listings—is not necessarily the most productive. For example, some people do find jobs through massive direct-mail campaigns (the targeting strategy carried to the extreme), but mass mailing is certainly one of the least effective job-search techniques.

Put at least half of your job-search efforts into networking. Do it carefully but eagerly. An estimated 65 to 70 percent of jobs are found through networking. As I noted in the Introduction, most people find jobs through friends, relatives, colleagues, classmates, and other acquaintances. The percentage is even greater for higher level positions. An estimated 80 percent of Harvard Business School alumni, for instance, find jobs through networking. The combination of the targeting and networking strategies can be particularly fruitful.

If you don't believe these statistics on networking, do your own polling. Describe the four primary search strategies to a number of friends and acquaintances, then ask how they found out about their current or previous jobs. Allow for the possibility of an "other" category to cover job fairs, on-campus interviews, and approaches outside of the four main strategies.

Do more than answer ads. Only 5 to 10 percent of jobs are found through help-wanted ads and other newspaper and on-line job postings. Despite these statistics, some job seekers put 80 to 90 percent of their efforts into this approach because it is the easiest strategy to implement. You should certainly respond to ads and other job listings that interest you, and put forward your best effort when responding.

Track your success rate for each strategy. Define *success* as the number of job interviews obtained. Assuming that you are using a somewhat balanced approach across the strategies (while emphasizing networking, of course), calculate what percentage of your job interviews come from each approach, and then emphasize the strategy or strategies that are working best for you, without completely abandoning the others.

NETWORKING

Networking is building relationships, asking for information or help, and looking for ways to provide value to the other person. You must work at the first aspect to be more effective at the second; that is why tapping into your existing network of friends and acquaintances is so important—the relationship already exists. But to be most effective in the job search, you need to expand your network beyond the people you already know. And to stand out in your networking, you need to make the third part of the definition operational by identifying and implementing ways to add value to those with whom you network, particularly people you had not previously known. Being remembered is good in networking, assuming that you are remembered in a positive rather than a negative way.

Starting Up

Contact managers whom you liked and worked well for and with, particularly those who have gone to other employers. Because these people know what you can do and have worked at multiple organizations themselves, reconnecting with them usually will provide you with good contacts.

Recent graduates should contact professors and alumni from their school (particularly alumni who were one or two years ahead and are now working; they remember well what it was like to be starting out). Also, tap into your parents' and your friends' parents' networks, even if they are unaware that they have networks.

Let everyone know you are looking for work. Include your immediate and extended family; your current and former co-workers, subordinates, and other professional associates; your friends, neighbors, former neighbors, and former classmates; your realtor, banker, lawyer, accountant, insurance agent, mechanic, and barber or hairdresser; your priest, minister, or rabbi; your doctor and dentist. Also include contacts from professional associations, social and sports club members, PTA members and faculty, parents of your children's friends, and anyone else who has given you a business card or to whom you have written a check in the past year. Develop a similar list from the contacts of your spouse/significant other/partner.

Perform the following activities energetically, thoughtfully, and frequently.

- Talk on the phone.

- Mail or fax letters or résumés.

- Send e-mail messages.

- Consider publishing occasional "news notes" to references, network contacts, and people with whom you have interviewed.

Use a referral name (or other connection, such as an alumni status) whenever possible—ideally for every contact you make. Most job seekers are more successful with warm calls than cold calls. Alumni status is no longer limited to academic institutions you attended. Alumni groups for former employers are on the rise.

Don't ask new network contacts if they have a job for you. Most of the time they will not, and the conversation will be over. Let those you contact off the hook immediately by stating that, although you currently are looking for work, you don't expect them to have a job for you. Your friends and network contacts are not likely to have a job immediately available anyway, so why put them on the spot?

People tend to be more willing and able to help you if they know you don't expect them to have a job for you. You are looking for any help these contacts might provide, be it ideas, job leads, or the names of *their* contacts, who could also be resources for you. Sometimes when you ask for help you will be told no or brushed off more politely. Most of the time, however, people will try to help you, particularly if you know them or if the referral name you use (or the connection you mention) means something to them.

If you make a good impression on your contacts, they will probably consider you for an appropriate position that becomes available in the future as long as you really did make a favorable impression and have kept in contact with them.

In the early stages of your search, express your needs to contacts in a very general way. You might tell them, "I'm looking for any help you might provide in my job search." Later you probably will want to be, and can be, much more specific in your requests.

- Ask contacts about a rumored job opening in their organization.

- Have them review the list of organizations you are targeting in your search.

- Ask them if they know anything about an organization, or hiring manager, with whom you are about to interview.

Build your network by telling people what you need from them, but, again, don't put them on the spot by asking them for a job.

Discuss your skills and how you have helped previous managers and organizations solve problems; don't simply cite your job titles. Use this approach in networking and in the job search in general. Focus on your accomplishments.

Ask friends and network contacts not to "circulate" your résumé, and gently resist requests to do so. Although this suggestion may seem counterintuitive, the key is maintaining control of your search process, as your job search never will be as important to others as it is to you. If people volunteer to distribute your résumé, unless they strongly insist, ask them instead for the names of the people they might distribute it to, so that you can contact these people directly (using the name of the person who referred you, of course). There will be some instances in which you agree to let someone "walk around" your résumé, but make these situations the exception, not the rule.

Learn more about job-search networking. Attend seminars or read some of the excellent books on the topic, such as the following:

- *Richard Beatty's Job Search Networking*

- *Power Networking: 55 Secrets for Personal and Professional Success,* by Donna Fisher and Sandy Vilas

- *Networking Skills That Will Get You the Job You Want,* by Cherie Kerr

- *Dig Your Well before You're Thirsty,* by Harvey Mackay

- *National Business Employment Weekly: Networking,* by Douglas B. Richardson

- *The Secrets of Savvy Networking,* by Susan RoAne

- *Networking for Everyone: Connecting with People for Career and Job Success,* by L. Michele Tullier

But remember, of course, that "it depends" is the answer to almost all questions in the job search, and certainly in the networking aspects of the search process.

Getting Out There

Network, network, network at

- professional, religious, social, and other organizations

- job-search support groups (if they exist in your area)

- business events open to the public (such as those sponsored by the Chamber of Commerce, the Rotary Club, and the Kiwanis Club)

- job fairs and company open houses

- organizations you belong to and ones you might want to join (go to meetings as a prospective member)

- anyplace people gather

Attend meetings of local chapters of professional organizations in your current discipline, or in one that you would like to consider. Usually you can participate as a nonmember, although you might have to pay an additional fee. Arrive in time for the social hour, often held before the formal meeting, and talk to people in your current or prospective field. These face-to-face contacts can be a great source of information and referrals. At these professional meetings, you will also meet other employed and unemployed job seekers from the same discipline; consider teaming up with them to help in one another's search. Try thinking of these fellow job seekers as compatriots rather than competitors.

Consider professional development programs as opportunities to increase your knowledge and skills, and to expand your network. If you are out of work and concerned about the expense involved, try to volunteer your services (perhaps working at a registration table) to get free or discounted access to the event.

Attend shorter programs and speeches in areas of interest. Such events might be sponsored by networking groups, adult and continuing education programs, alumni associations, professional and trade associations, and community and governmental organizations. Make contact with speakers, attendees, and program sponsors.

Search the business sections of major local papers and local business journals for columns listing events of possible interest. (For example, in the Sunday *Boston Globe* business section, Juliet Brudney's "Living with Work" column includes a list of career development events for the upcoming week, and *The Boston Business Journal* publishes an even more extensive list near the back of every weekly issue.)

Pursue and establish connections with authors of articles and books in your field. Perhaps the best way to start is by sending a letter of introduction or similar e-mail message. If you make the effort, you can connect with some extremely interesting, often inspiring, and perhaps even helpful people as part of your job-search process. Consider developing and using your personal "standard networking letter" for this purpose (see below).

Contact local elected officials to let them know of your background and your current job search. Local council members, mayors, state representatives, state senators, and U.S. representatives are there to serve their constituents; they have numerous contacts in your area. Meet with these elected officials (or their local staff) to let them know what kind of work you are looking for. Leave a copy of your résumé for their reference, but indicate that you would prefer to be referred to people with whom you can follow up, rather than have these officials distribute your résumé. Again, you want to stay in control of the search process.

Accept help. If a friend or contact suggests that you talk to a person who, at first glance, does not seem to have anything to offer, talk to this person anyway.

Be patient and open to hearing "no." Not everyone will be able or willing to help you. For every contact who will not help, numerous others will.

Read newspaper, magazine, and trade journal columns featuring recently hired or promoted professionals. Consider contacting them, even with a cold call. Congratulate them, and then explain that you are currently searching for a job, and see if you can get their help. Newly hired professionals are often not overly busy for the first few weeks (or even months), so perhaps they would even agree to meet with you. A word of caution: Sometimes these formal announcements are published long after the actual event, so by the time you contact those listed, they may be fully engaged in their new job.

Try to get in front of people, if possible, but always be respectful of their time. If you request and get a meeting with a network contact, keep it short and make the best use of the time. Also, remember that many of those currently employed are working long hours and may not have time for a face-to-face meeting, particularly during work hours, but they still may be helpful in your search. If you think it critical to get in front of someone too busy to meet you at their office, invite the person out for breakfast, lunch, or dinner.

If you asked for "twenty minutes" when you set up a networking appointment, at the eighteen- or nineteen-minute mark, remind the person that the time you requested is almost up. Let the person say that it is okay to keep going, but be ready to stop if he or she does not. Follow up on each of these meetings with the near-mandatory thank-you letter (or e-mail message), and then keep these people informed about your search process.

Keep notes on all the referrals you receive, even those you do not contact immediately. When you do contact these people, they usually will not know (or care) if you were given their name recently or months ago, so don't feel guilty if you are not following up on referrals promptly. The exception is when the person providing the contact name tells you that he or she soon will call the referral to "introduce" you. In that case, you do need to follow up with the contact promptly.

Keep track of network contacts. Whether you do so on paper or by computer, use a system that is easily updated and includes

- name
- whom you were referred by (or other connection)
- title and company/organization name
- address, including zip code
- telephone and fax numbers
- e-mail address
- secretary/administrative assistant's name and telephone number
- date(s) contacted
- notes on conversation(s)
- date of planned *next* contact

Previously mentioned computer applications, such as ACT, Lotus Organizer, and Microsoft Outlook have contact organizers that can be extremely helpful in the networking data management process.

Whatever system or approach you use for networking data management, make sure that maintaining the system does not interfere with other, more important job-search activities. One way is to work on the system only at nights and on weekends—"off" hours in the job search.

Share your personal network. Refer jobs you uncover to fellow job seekers, supply network contacts to others, and provide additional help. Again, think of these fellow job seekers as compatriots rather than competitors.

Other Networking Tips (and Tools)

Break the "networking barrier." Think of your network as a tree diagram with the people you currently know as "Level 0" and those they refer you to as "Level 1." In your networking, get at least to "Level 2" and ideally beyond (contacting people referred to you by someone you hadn't known when you started your current job search). Most job seekers do not break this networking barrier because they feel they do not "know" the Level 1 people they contact, and thus greatly curtail the speed at which they could be expanding their network.

Build your network both vertically and horizontally. Do it vertically by breaking the networking barrier just described, and horizontally by getting more referrals from those who previously gave you names. Try to get at least two referrals from each person you talk with, but, because some contacts will not provide any names, aim for an average of two referrals among all the people you contact in your networking efforts. (One networking contact to whom I was referred—a Level 1 contact—provided me with thirty-two names and numbers, along with background information on each person, the first time I got in touch with him.)

One way to get more names from previous contacts is to demonstrate to them that you are following up on their referrals; another is giving something back to these previous contacts.

Create a "standard networking letter." This letter (of not more than a page) can be used to accompany a résumé that you send to people you have met or networked with by phone, or you can use it to contact speakers from presentations you have attended or authors of good books or articles you have read.

- The first paragraph should be unique and relate to the conversation you had, or it should thank or commend the person for an excellent presentation, book, article, and so forth.

- The rest of the letter is the "standard" part. It tells or reminds the recipient who you are, why you are in the job market, and what you are looking for; it also asks for help, or additional help, and tells the person that you will follow up with a phone call in a few weeks.

- Make the standard part of this letter a template that you revise as necessary; then be sure to customize each networking letter you send.

- Some job seekers prefer to contact those to whom they have been referred by letter first, rather than by phone. Your standard networking letter also could be used for that purpose.

Treat initial network contacts in an appropriate manner, so that they will feel comfortable that you will do the same with anyone to

whom they refer you. A common approach in networking with people you do not know but have been referred to is to start with a phone call. Make it a short one. Unless it is very clear that the person wants to talk longer, after no more than five to ten minutes, ask if you could send the contact a copy of your résumé. (Be forewarned—the person often will say yes just to get you off the phone.)

That day, send your standard networking letter along with your résumé. Follow up in a few weeks with a second call, hoping that the person remembers you but being prepared to re-introduce yourself.

It is much more appropriate to ask for (and you are more likely to receive) networking referrals on this follow-up call, because you have demonstrated through your actions (the initial short call and the businesslike follow-up letter and résumé) that you understand how to network properly. The person contacted is now somewhat assured that you also will treat any contacts he or she provides in an appropriate manner, and thus may be more willing to supply his or her "better" contacts when asked.

Build a networking paper trail. When you write a letter to a referral, send a copy of the letter to the person who originally referred you. Add to the letter a short, handwritten note thanking the person for his or her help and indicating that you will let the person know what happens with the contact. This gesture is not only the polite thing to do, but it also may result in more referrals from that person now or later (building your networking horizontally).

Add value. Again, networking is building relationships, asking for information or help, and *looking for ways to provide value to the other person.* The third part of the definition is the key to successful and productive networking. Job seekers often wonder what possible value they could provide to others, particularly those who are employed. Here are some ideas:

- If you have something in your files that a network contact could use, get it to the person as quickly as possible.

- If you later spot an article that might be of interest to someone you previously contacted, mail, fax, or e-mail a copy with a note such as, "FYI—thought you might be interested."

- If you uncover information that may help a network contact's business, let the person know immediately. If you give a potential lead to the independent consultants in your network, they will be in your debt forever.

- If you are in a position to help children of network contacts in some way (for instance, with their job search if they are recent college graduates), do so. This approach is particularly well suited to more senior level people with whom you network, as it seems harder to "help" them.

By starting out with the intent of always looking for ways to add value, you will come up with some creative ways, and, more important, the people with whom you network will sense your attitude and respond very favorably to it.

Stay in touch with network contacts. Communicate with them regularly but not so often as to pester them. Vary the way you stay in contact—do not always call. Consider sending a networking letter, an e-mail message, or even a postcard to bring them up to date on your search status. Or call and ask to leave a voice mail message rather than talking to them directly, and make sure the message is short.

Keep on the lookout for good additions to your network. When you find them, be sure to introduce them to others to strengthen the ties between you and those in your network. An out-of-work human resources manager I once met identified around twenty people who had been extremely helpful to him in his job search. He then asked these people if they would be willing to have their names and contact information shared with the others in this helpful group. They all said yes, so he distributed to each person the complete list of names and contact information.

Use your network as it was intended, and make sure those in it get back from you as much as, or more than, they give. Job seekers who take but do not give may have short-term success, but their reputations eventually will catch up with them.

TARGETING ORGANIZATIONS

Targeting is the most frequently overlooked, and underused, job-search strategy. The goal is *not* to select one thousand companies, then aim a direct-mail campaign at them. Rather, it is to be constantly trying to identify organizations that might interest you as potential employers, then attempting to network into the organizations directly or into the search firms that are placing people in these targeted employers.

For senior-level executives, targeting is critical because there are fewer jobs at their level. Extensive research is required to identify appropriate positions that are open, about to be open, or perhaps need to be open because of poor company performance. Targeting can be fruitful for candidates at all levels, because it gives the job seeker some control.

Know your target industry (or industries) thoroughly. What are industry trends? Are potential employers growing or downsizing? Which ones are on the way up or on the way down, and why? An organization in turmoil or going through downsizing could be an excellent job-search target. Good people leave firms in these situations, thus creating opportunities. Such a company is probably not going to offer you job security, but then no companies do anymore. Because an organization in trouble is often short of key skills in many areas, you might pick up valuable experience, sometimes in areas to which you might not have access in a more stable environment.

Identify organizations you might consider working for based on your specific criteria. The criteria might include industry, type of organization, size, growth potential, organization culture, location, length of commute, family-friendly orientation, or any combination of these or other factors appropriate to your personal situation.

Develop and maintain a target-company list, and then try to network into the organizations on your list. Most job seekers never attempt to implement a targeting strategy; this omission is a mistake, and a serious one.

If your target list is short (three to four firms), ask everyone in your existing network (or anyone else you meet or communicate with by phone or e-mail) if he or she knows anyone at these firms. Many job seekers who do targeting will develop a longer target list, but a workable number is no more than fifteen to twenty-five organizations. Show the list to everyone you know or meet, and fax, mail, or e-mail it to your references and others in your network. Update your target list regularly, adding new employers as you identify them and dropping those that are no longer of interest. Some on the list could even change daily; in a sense, the specific names listed are not as important as the process of working to identify these employers on a continuing basis.

Think twice before considering a mass mailing, but if you decide to go ahead with one, make it targeted. The expected return rate on mass mailings in the job search is about 1 percent (for every 1,000 letters you send by mail, you will perhaps get 10 responses). For most job seekers, this is an expensive, time-consuming, and unproductive technique. The better you target, however, the higher the likely return.

Although targeted mass mailings can play a role in the job search, this technique should not be the first approach you use. And don't do a mass mailing, targeted or otherwise, because you are out of work and an outplacement service you have been provided supports this effort or, even worse, because other job seekers you know seem to be doing similar mailings. Targeted mailings can, however, be an effective technique to broadcast your availability to retained search firms, particularly if you are flexible about relocation.

Be sure to follow up on all the letters you send. Remember that, because of all the other job-search activities you will be performing, there is a practical limit to the number of letters you can effectively follow up on by phone—perhaps twenty-five to fifty per week—and this is if you are out of work and searching for a job full time.

USING AGENCIES AND SEARCH FIRMS

Search firms work well for some job seekers (primarily those who have a clear focus and marketable skills and experience in a specific area) and not at all for others. Don't take it personally if you are in the latter category; consider it one of those job-search indignities mentioned in Chapter 5.

If a search firm will not present you as a candidate to its current client company or companies, that does not mean you are unemployable. You just do not meet that search firm's criteria for the specific search(es) currently being conducted.

Be aware that the terminology in this area of the job search can be very confusing. People sometimes call the different types of firms by different names. For example, what is a *headhunter*? Originally it applied to retained search professionals who reached into organizations to try to "steal" current employees. Now the term is generally used more generically to apply to all search firms. But some people use *search firms* generically, whereas others use it to mean only retained search firms. Finally, temporary placement once applied only to manufacturing workers and office administrative personnel, but now temps are being placed at all levels in organizations, including the executive suite.

Recognize the difference between **retained** *and* **contingency** *search firms and use them appropriately.* *Retained search firms* normally have an exclusive relationship with an employer for a search they are conducting for a specific position (and for a certain time period). These firms typically receive a fee of one-third of the first year's salary of the person to be hired, and they get paid for their efforts whether or not they fill the position (thus the word *retained,* as in a sense these firms are paid consultants). Of course, such firms will not get much repeat business from a client company if they fail to meet that company's needs by filling the job (or at least finding acceptable candidates).

Contingency search firms occasionally have an exclusive relationship with an employer, but more typically they are in competition with other contingency firms. The employer pays this type of search firm only after an applicant they have submitted accepts the position. These firms typically receive a fee of 20 to 25 percent of the first year's salary of the person being hired, and they agree to return the fee (possibly in cash but more likely in equivalent services) if the placed person leaves the new position too quickly (for instance, within ninety days).

Retained firms probably will not want to speak with you, or see you, unless they are currently seeking someone exactly matching your skills, knowledge, experience, and education. These firms primarily deal with positions above a certain salary level ($100K or higher is the minimum amount often mentioned), although they may occasionally handle lower level positions as a favor to a client company. Some retained firms deal strictly with very senior-level positions. Again, you should not be surprised if retained firms ignore you, unless they are conducting a specific search for which you would be a potential candidate.

Some contingency firms do retained searches on occasion, and some retained firms will do contingency work (although the latter would rarely admit it).

Never forget that both retained and contingency search firms are working for (get paid by) the employer; they are not working for you. This does not mean that these firms cannot or will not help, but remember where their primary interests lie. Do let the search professional run interference for you with a potential employer, however, about salary, benefits, perks, and other issues.

Also remember that search firms primarily place people experienced in a field, industry, and so forth. Few of their client firms would be willing to pay a search fee for an inexperienced person or a career changer. So if you are a recent graduate or career changer, concentrate on networking and don't expect search firms to be very helpful.

Never pay the placement fee of a contingency search firm. Years ago candidates sometimes paid, but now the vast majority of reputable search firms are company-paid.

Use networking as the best way to identify good agencies and search firms with which to deal. Think about the search firms, and individual search professionals, that you (or organizations that you work for or have worked for) have used. Ask network contacts and other job seekers which firm(s), and which specific contacts at each firm, they would recommend. If the same names are mentioned repeatedly, you will know that these are good search firms or search consultants to work with. Getting the names of individual search professionals is much more valuable than just the name of a firm, as the search field is very person-dependent.

Also use published directories to find agencies and search firms. *The Directory of Executive Recruiters*, commonly known as "the Red Book" and published annually by Kennedy Information, is the best-known and most widely available directory of this type. It can be found in most libraries and in an increasing number of bookstores or ordered directly from the publisher by calling 800-531-0007. The number of similar search-firm directories available in bookstores (almost all less expensive) seems to be constantly increasing. These include *Job Seekers' Guide to Executive Recruiters,* by Christopher H. Hunt and Scott A. Scanlon, and, by the same authors, *Job Seekers' Guide to Wall Street Recruiters* and *Job Seekers' Guide to Silicon Valley Recruiters.* Kennedy Information also publishes the *International Directory of Executive Recruiters.*

A smaller, companion paperback to the Red Book, *Kennedy's Pocket Guide to Working with Executive Recruiters,* is useful regardless of whether you are an "executive." Among the valuable points it makes is not to take rejection by search firms personally.

Another book that extensively discusses the retained search business is the previously mentioned *The New Rules of Passage at*

$100,000+: The Insider's Lifetime Guide to Executive Job-Changing and Faster Career Progress, by John Lucht. It includes an appendix with more than three hundred retained search firms that Lucht identifies as outstanding.

Most books that list search firms do not evaluate them. Another one that does, however, is *The New Career Makers,* by John Sibbald. He selects and describes what he considers the 250 best search professionals in the United States.

For those interested in executive- or professional-level temporary assignments, Kennedy Information publishes *The Directory of Temporary Placement Firms for Executives, Managers, and Professionals* (discussed in Chapter 5). Two recent books that discuss this growing phenomenon are *Executive Temping: A Guide for Professionals,* by Saralee Terry Woods, and *Executive Temp,* by Diane Thrailkill.

Select a core group of search firms with which to try to work; then consider broadening your circle. Finding the right set of agencies and search firms is time consuming; this process includes personal referrals, other research, personal interviews, and inspection. When you have found an agency or search firm that seems right, try to get referred in by using the name of someone familiar to the search firm—ideally someone for whom the agency or firm has completed a search assignment. If you cannot get referred in, ask in writing for a personal interview and follow up with a phone call. But again, don't be surprised if search professionals, particularly from retained firms, don't want to meet with you.

If you are a senior-level individual contributor or a mid- to senior-level manager, consider doing a targeted mailing to nationwide retained search firms that specialize in your field, particularly if you are willing to relocate. Like all mass mailings in the job search, the response rate will not be high, but you might get lucky and contact a retained firm that has a search in progress for a position matching your skills and experience. You may even uncover a distant search firm that has been retained to fill a position that matches your skills and experience and is also in your area.

Make sure your references are set before contacting agencies and search firms. These firms may want to check references at the start of the process to help determine if they will represent you to their client companies.

Be explicit about your current or last salary, any salary requirements, and your location preference(s) when communicating with agencies and search firms. These firms, particularly contingency search firms, treat potential candidates less as people and more as products to be placed in one or more "boxes" (as defined by the marketplace). Search firms normally want to know your salary requirements and relocation flexibility to determine how realistic your expectations are and if it will be worth representing you. If you truly are flexible about salary, let the firm or agency know that.

If a search firm contacts you, ask questions to determine its legitimacy and credibility. Find out if the firm is contingency or retainer, if it is working on an exclusive assignment, if it has any professional affiliations, and where its main office is located.

See what a search firm will do to your résumé. Ask to look at what will be sent to prospective employers. Is their version (if they modify it) a good representation of you and what you have to offer?

Ask to be contacted by a contingency firm before your materials are submitted to a prospective employer. This advice is fairly standard to avoid potential conflicts caused by more than one contingency firm submitting your résumé, or the firm being in competition with a submission that you made on your own. Your need to make this request may depend on the relationship you have with the contingency firm, your primary contact there, and your trust in that person's judgment.

Try to develop an ongoing relationship with search professionals. Periodically update them on new pertinent skills you have acquired and the status of your search. If possible, get so well networked with other job seekers in your discipline or industry that search consultants call you to ask if you know anyone for a position they have available. Beware, however, that those in the search field often use this approach as a ploy when what they really want is to determine if you are interested in a position they have available.

RESPONDING TO ADS AND OTHER JOB POSTINGS

Some people do find jobs through classified ads and other job postings, including the ever-increasing number of jobs listed on-line. The main reason to avoid making ad responses your primary or only search strategy, however, is to avoid constantly fighting a numbers game. Because ads and Internet postings are widely available and job seekers can access them inexpensively, the number of respondents is often large. Some applicants will be determined totally unqualified, but their material still must be reviewed (or at least scanned). Responding to ads and other postings is not an unwinnable approach, but the odds against you are significant.

Respond to any classified ad that comes close to matching your skills and interests. It doesn't have to be an exact match, as ads and other job postings usually describe the firm's ideal candidate. Don't be disappointed or disillusioned, however, if you get no response to a great percentage of the ads or other job postings to which you respond: The employer or search firm listing the position may receive a large number of replies.

Read ads carefully for the information you can glean about industries, specific organizations, and what is happening in the overall marketplace. If you are new to the job market, review the Sunday help-wanted section for the past two to three months in the major newspapers in your area or in any area to which you would consider relocating. Look not necessarily for specific jobs (although previously advertised positions might still be open), but to see what organizations have been hiring and to identify employers that might be of interest.

If you are interested in a previously advertised job, contact the organization and ask if a candidate has been chosen. Perhaps the job was put on hold and is about to be re-opened, the person hired did not work out, or the firm has experienced so much growth that additional opportunities are now available.

Think about how quickly you should respond to newspaper ads. Opinions about this timing issue vary widely. Some people feel that the response should be immediate; others think it best to wait a few days to a week or two, so that your résumé will arrive after the initial deluge of responses. Probably the best rule of thumb is this: The smaller the ad, the more quickly you should respond. If it has been two or more weeks since the ad ran, you might call the hiring organization, simply to ask if it is still accepting applications. Why waste time crafting an outstanding letter that will go immediately into the trash because the employer is no longer accepting résumés?

In contrast, respond as soon as possible to Internet job postings. Speed is everything on-line.

Consider scanning the* National Ad Search Weekly, *which lists ads from major newspapers across the country. This publication's best feature is its grouping of jobs according to discipline (for instance, all management training jobs are listed together). A word of caution, however: The listing company has no idea that this publication has copied the ad from whatever newspaper it paid to have the ad published in. Thus you should not apply to a nonlocal firm under the assumption that the firm will be willing to pay relocation costs. The equivalent of this publication is also available at various Internet sites, and, naturally, the publication now has its own Web site: <www.nationaladsearch.com>.

Get all the information you can from the ad (and elsewhere) before responding, and then write a unique cover letter focused on the needs expressed. Use this approach even if you start the process by copying one of your previous letters, or recycling a set of paragraphs from various letters. Make each letter the best you can, because even though many screeners scan the résumé first to see if there is a possible fit before reading the cover letter, some may look at the letter first.

Look for any special instructions or other information provided. These could include application deadlines, directions not to telephone, or indications that résumés will be scanned electronically. "Principals only" or "principals until [date]" means that the hiring organization does not want to be contacted by search firms at all, or only on or after the date specified. The organization is making it clear that it would prefer not to pay a contingency placement fee.

Reference the ad you are responding to in your cover letter, and note where you found the ad. Include publication name and date. The hiring organization may have run the ad in multiple places and thus be interested in knowing where you found it.

Respond directly to the hiring manager if possible. If the name is not provided in the ad, try to determine it through your network. If that approach fails, consider calling the employer and asking for the name of the hiring manager and the human resources person involved (unless the ad says not to call about the job). If possible, send separate letters to both the hiring manager and the human resources contact (or one letter to the former with a "cc" to the latter).

If you cannot get a name from the ad or elsewhere, consider eliminating the salutation and replacing it with an "in reference to" ("re:") line. Place this line just above the first paragraph of your letter (for example, "Re: Ad in *The Boston Globe*, April 2, 2000, for a Customer Service Manager").

Respond to each ad with a personalized letter and a copy of your résumé. Your cover letter should include

- the purpose of the letter and enclosed résumé;
- the qualifications you bring to the job/organization, clearly and persuasively matched with those specified;
- a statement of why you want to work for the organization;
- a follow-up plan, specifying the easiest way(s) and best time(s) to reach you; and
- an indication that you will call the organization if you do not hear from it within a reasonable time.

Some job seekers responding to ads and other job postings include two columns in the middle section of their cover letter, with the left column labeled "Your Requirements" and the right one labeled "My Experience." Then they put appropriate bullets under each label matching their background with what the ad specifically asks for. That approach certainly makes it easier for the screener/reviewer, but it will only help applicants who meet (or exceed) all (or most) of the stated requirements. Even if you do not use this two-column format, consider the concept involved, helping to make it easier for the screener to accept rather than reject your application.

If salary requirements or history are requested, ignore the request or, even better, include a sentence such as "My salary requirements are negotiable and can be discussed at the interview." Specific responses to salary requests are used primarily to screen out candidates, but most screeners will not eliminate you from consideration if you don't respond to this request with specifics (if you are otherwise a viable candidate).

If a single ad lists several jobs that interest you, write a customized letter in response to each job advertised. If there are two or more attractive jobs listed in one ad, write separate, focused letters for each job, perhaps mailing them a few days apart. You may get called for both positions. If you apply for two unrelated jobs with the same letter, you will seem less interested in either position.

When responding to a "blind ad," write a good cover letter, mail or fax it, file it in your blind ad folder, and then forget about it. A blind ad gives a box or fax number but does not indicate the listing company's name. The odds are very low that you will get a response to this type of ad. If you get a call from an employer or an agency you did not contact, ask how the organization got your résumé. It might have been through your response to a blind ad. Be cautious about applying to this type of ad if you are employed: Your employer may have run the ad.

7

Special Topics

T<small>HE THREE TOPICS</small> addressed in this chapter do not apply to all job seekers but will to some. *Long-distance job searches* are more difficult to conduct but certainly not impossible to complete successfully. *Job fairs* can be very helpful for many job seekers but are probably not useful for those at a more senior level. The issue of *age discrimination* weighs heavily on the minds of many older job seekers, but, unfortunately, some use it as an excuse for their lack of success in the search process.

DOING A LONG-DISTANCE JOB SEARCH

Complicated logistics and the fact that most people will not have established networks at their desired locations make long-distance searches especially demanding. In looking for a job in a location at a distance from you, perform the activities suggested in this book but in an even more organized and systematic manner.

Thoroughly research the new location. Contact the local chamber of commerce and any other community, professional, and alumni organizations in the new area. Not only will you get access to published information, Web sites, and so forth, but you might also make personal contacts in these organizations—people who might help in your search efforts.

Make use of any alumni connections. As recommended in Chapter 5, contact the alumni office or career center at any college or university you attended. Find out if any alumni have volunteered to serve as network contacts for fellow alums in the job search. These individuals can be particularly helpful for those considering a move to a new area. Also find out if an alumni directory is available in print or on-line. See if a staff person has been designated as the alumni career advisor. Sometimes this advisory service is provided by the on-campus career center; other times it is part of the alumni office. Try both places.

Plan an extended trip or several day-long trips to your new location (if financially and logistically feasible) and make some appointments before you go. If you do not preschedule your meetings, some of the people with whom you want to meet may be out of town during your visit. Be sure, however, to leave some open slots in your visit calendar to take advantage of any opportunities that arise.

Use to your advantage the fact that some people at the new location might be more willing to help you than they would a local job seeker. This is so because (1) people will want you, as a newcomer, to have a good impression of their area, and (2) they might have done, or know someone who has done, a long-distance job search and realize how difficult and frustrating it can be.

JOB FAIRS

Job seekers up to, but probably not including, the executive level should attend job fairs and open houses held by employers. Although these events, particularly the larger ones, may feel like meat markets, employers would not spend the money to participate in job fairs or organize open houses if they did not consider them a good source of potential candidates. In addition to the jobs available, the networking possibilities with employer representatives and other attendees and the variety of written information available on participating or sponsoring organizations make these events worthwhile.

Preparing

Don't expect to be hired on the spot, although occasionally you can get a formal interview during one of these events. View a job fair as a chance to gather data on participating employers and the overall job

market, to network with organization representatives and other attendees, and possibly to stumble on a job or a job lead.

*Before attending, find out what employers plan to be there, and do
research on them.* Advance preparation saves time by letting you target the organizations that most interest you.

*Reduce your one- to two-minute introduction to a focused twenty- to
thirty-second statement.* State clearly and concisely your work experience, a few key accomplishments, and your goals.

Take twice as many résumés as there are exhibitors. You will need
one résumé to leave at the exhibit booth or table, and an additional
copy for anyone at the booth with whom you have a meaningful conversation (to help avoid your résumé getting lost in the large stack
headed for the human resources department).

*Bring your personal business cards to trade with employer represen-
tatives and for networking with other attendees.* You meet many
people in the job search, and at job fairs you may meet a large number of them in a relatively short period. Leave them something to
remember you by, and try to get their business cards as well so that
you can follow up on your conversation.

Dress for business. You may meet your next boss at a booth—or he or
she may be waiting in line with you. Don't let anyone's first impression of you be less than professional.

*Carry a note pad and a pen, preferably in a leather folder, for a busi-
nesslike look.* Do not bring your briefcase if possible.

Participating

*Arrive early and, before entering, get the finalized list of participat-
ing employers.* The original roster of employers may have been
changed. Identify your target organizations and prioritize them. Go to
these employers in order of your preference, but also visit every booth
if possible; do not rule yourself out.

Be selective about information you supply on any registration form.
Anything provided on the form, even if handwritten (for example, your
responses to questions about previous salary or salary requirements),

may get scanned in along with your résumé. This information thus will be available to participating employers and to other organizations who pay the job fair organizer for an electronic copy.

Know what you are there for and get it: Be active, not passive. The customary exchange of information at a job fair is not the equivalent of an interview. Your focus should be on making contacts, collecting information, and trying to get invited back to the employer for a real interview. Also be aware that some of the employer representatives at these events may be contract recruiters rather than company employees.

Talk to someone at every booth or table. Because the employers are selling their opportunities, you have a slight advantage. Ask questions about the organization—what it does and how it is doing—before talking about yourself. This approach allows you to tailor subsequent comments and to present yourself in the most favorable light.

Show a strong interest. Ask for literature, for an assessment of where the organization is going, for information on company history/culture/decision making, and so forth.

Allow an exchange of information about you without letting the recruiters monopolize the time. Depending on the length of the waiting lines, assume that you have no more than a few minutes to give each employer representative you speak with a good sense of who you are and to get what you need.

Ask for information about the hiring process and identify the next step(s). As in all areas of the job search, the more you know—in this case about the employer's future plans—the better off you will be, even if things don't work out as planned.

Collect business cards from everyone you talk with. You then can follow up by letter, phone call, or e-mail when the representatives are not so harried.

Arrange specific times to follow up with each employer that expresses interest in you or on which you are interested. You might say, for example, "Ms. Manager, I realize you are very busy today, but your company sounds exciting and I would like to speak with you further about employment possibilities there. Can we set up a time in the next few days when we could meet or when I could call you?"

Leave each employer's booth or table with the following:

- Annual reports, brochures, and so forth

- Position descriptions (if available)

- Company culture and decision-making information

- The name of the person to contact to follow up (name, position, phone number, and extension) and a specific time to contact him or her

Following Up

On leaving a booth, and at the end of the fair, go through your notes while things are still fresh in your mind. Review each organization and the possibilities that it may hold for you. Also consider the organizations as a whole, and what you might glean about industry trends, marketplace shifts, and long-term staffing needs.

Make additional notes or, even better, tape-record your observations, thoughts, and impressions. Ideally, do the recording as soon as possible on an easily transportable microcassette recorder. Your first impressions can be extremely valuable and may be lost if not captured as soon, and in as much detail, as possible.

Soon after the fair, reprioritize your target company list and determine your next steps. Nothing may happen unless you help make it happen. Avoid having your résumé disappear in an organizational "black hole." Because these companies are participating in the job fair or hosting the open house you can generally assume that they are hiring, so take the initiative and try to get the interview back at their location.

OVERCOMING AGE DISCRIMINATION

Does age discrimination exist in the hiring process? Of course it does, but you probably know some seventy-year-olds who act thirty and some thirty-year-olds who act seventy. Your attitude is the key to overcoming this type of discrimination. It is also important, however, to know when to turn away from a specific job or organization because the odds are stacked against you, and refocus on an employer or an area in which you are more likely to have success.

Avoid using age discrimination as an excuse for lack of success in your job search. Certainly discrimination may be a factor, but too many older job seekers leap to the conclusion that their age is the problem when it may be their experience, the way they present themselves, or their less-than-positive attitude.

Look for situations in which your extensive experience would put you at an advantage. Many organizations, particularly smaller ones, can greatly benefit from your wealth of knowledge and experience. For example, Internet start-ups have a growing need for "adult supervision." The smaller the organization, however, the more likely that the position will be filled by networking. So you need to use networking to get to the people already employed in these smaller firms.

Identify specific, practical considerations that might make you more attractive to an organization, particularly a smaller one. For example, let it be known if you are willing and able to compromise on issues such as status and salary, and if you can tap into the benefits program of your spouse or some other source.

Recognize that there are battles you cannot win. If you sense that the bias against you is too strong because of age or any other reason, stop banging your head against the wall and move on to something more productive.

Consider taking a temporary or contract position. Temporary/contract workers are in demand at all organizational levels, and age is usually much less of an issue for these positions. People interested in executive- or professional-level temporary assignments should consult *The Directory of Temporary Placement Firms for Executives, Managers, and Professionals* (published by Kennedy Information).

Don't wait for the government to address the age discrimination issue. When older job seekers get frustrated with the search process and the barriers they encounter, they often demand that the government do something about this discrimination problem. Even if something is eventually done, the wheels of government work so slowly that it will not help the individual job seeker's situation.

Don't sue or think about suing, even for blatant examples of age discrimination. Although perhaps justified, these legal actions would divert your focus from where it needs to be—on doing everything you can to determine the needs of employers and hiring managers and positioning yourself to meet those needs.

8

Interviews

ALL YOUR HARD WORK in your job search has got you to this critical stage. Congratulations! Now you have a face-to-face opportunity to convince a hiring manager, and probably other interviewers, that you are the right person to address their needs. And it is at this stage that job seekers most often mishandle the opportunity. Don't let that happen to you.

This chapter covers everything you will need to know to prepare for, perform well in, and follow up on interviews. But practice is the key in interviewing. The more job interviews you have, the better you likely will get at this critical aspect of the search process. And at this stage *success* means getting the job offer, or at least being selected for the next round of interviews.

GENERAL PREPARATION

Prepare for interviews by reviewing commonly asked questions and thinking about your responses. For example:

- "Tell me about yourself."

- "Why did you leave your last job?" or "Why do you want to leave your current job?"

- "Describe your strengths and weaknesses."

- "Why have you held so many jobs?" or "Why have you worked so long for one employer?"

- "Describe your relationship with your last three bosses."

- "What were your three biggest accomplishments in your last job? the job before that? your career so far?"

- "What is the biggest error you ever made in a work setting?"

- "If you could do anything differently in your career, what would it be?"

- "What do you know about our organization? our industry?"

- "Why do you want to work for us?"

- "What interests you the most about the position we have? the least?"

- "What are your salary expectations?"

- "Why should we hire you?"

You don't have to create and memorize standard responses to these or other possible interview questions, but it is extremely helpful to consider possible responses. You don't want to feel, or even worse act, blindsided by an interviewer's question, particularly if it is one you could have foreseen.

Read through even more extensive question lists in job-search books (or in outplacement manuals if you are out of work and receiving outplacement services). Some good books on interviewing include

- *The Complete Q & A Job Interview Book,* by Jeffrey G. Allen

- *The Five-Minute Interview,* by Richard H. Beatty

- *The Perfect Interview: How to Get the Job You Really Want,* by John D. Drake

- *National Business Employment Weekly: Interviewing,* by Arlene S. Hirsch

- *Sweaty Palms: The Neglected Art of Interviewing,* by H. Anthony Medley

- *Knock 'Em Dead,* by Martin Yate

Republished yearly, Yate's text is probably the best-selling book on interviewing (although it also covers all of the job search). It has spawned a veritable industry that includes *Résumés That Knock 'Em Dead* and *Cover Letters That Knock 'Em Dead.*

Create your own list of questions that you may feel uncomfortable answering. The key is to identify questions that might be difficult for you, then to predetermine and practice (but not word-for-word memorize) concise, to-the-point responses. This way you will feel confident going into each interview, even if these questions are never asked. A good friend or, even better, a more objective career or job-search counselor, can be very helpful in coaching you to develop, or modify, answers to questions that you perceive as difficult.

Accept every interview that is offered to you, particularly early in your job search. Meet with employers even if you are not very interested in the position or their organization. Interviewing involves a set of skills, and the more you practice these skills, the sharper they will become. Once you are successful in getting numerous first-round interviews, then you can start to be more selective about the interviews you accept. By accepting every interview, however, you may discover opportunities that you would have ruled out because of preconceived notions.

Remember that internal interviewing (that is, interviewing for a different position in the organization for which you work) is usually different from external interviewing. In many cases, your reputation will have preceded you, and the interviewer often will be trying to sell you on the position. And, at a minimum, the interviewer will assume you to be a cultural fit because you already work for the organization. If you have done a lot of internal interviewing, you still need to practice for the more difficult external interview—and to be particularly careful not to inadvertently drift into the generally more informal and friendly internal interviewing style.

Have a practice interview videotaped. Practice sessions can be done with a career counselor, an outplacement consultant, or anyone experienced in providing feedback about interview performance. Through this exercise, job seekers usually identify minor points they can easily correct and other areas that might need additional work. As a result, they become more confident in subsequent interviews.

Although you may never experience it, be prepared for a group interview (one with a panel of three or more interviewers). Make sure you know who the panelists are. If they do not introduce themselves and their organizational roles at the start (and you have not been provided this information ahead of time), attempt to get this information (ask them) before they begin asking you questions.

One way of handling a group interview is to answer each question by first addressing the questioner and then checking in (making eye contact) with each of the other panelists, ending your response by looking at the original questioner. Another way is to concentrate on the individual asking the question, blocking out the others until you have completed your response, and then making yourself available for questions from the other panelists.

Be prepared for and willing to take one or more pre-selection tests. Some organizations, or groups within organizations, require job-skill or psychological tests as part of the interviewing process, relying on them to provide a more well-rounded perspective on a candidate. Requiring these tests is fine as long as they are given to all applicants to an organization or to everyone applying for certain types or levels of jobs.

In taking psychological tests, carefully read the test instructions and answer the questions honestly—don't try to second-guess the "best" answers. Most often these tests are given to help determine if you are a good cultural match for the organization or work group.

BEFORE A SPECIFIC INTERVIEW

Besides any general preparation you do for the interviewing process, you need to adequately prepare for each new organization with which, and each position for which, you interview.

When an interview is set up, ask with whom you will be meeting and how long you should expect to be there. Be prepared and willing to stay longer. If possible, get the interviewers' names, titles, and roles. By asking, you may be able to find out, for example, that you will be meeting with a panel of interviewers, so that you will not be surprised to discover that situation as the interview begins.

If you are to be taken to lunch as part of an interviewing process, consider lunchtime part of the interview. Don't let your guard down.

To preserve your interviewing energy and enthusiasm, try not to schedule interviews with more than two different employers in one day: One in the morning and another in the afternoon or evening is plenty. Preparing for, traveling to, and going through an interview can be physically and emotionally taxing, and you want to be at your best in each interview.

Ask why **you** *were selected to be interviewed out of all the potential candidates.* The goal is to get an employer representative to articulate what the organization's hiring manager or screener(s) liked about you; this information might be different from what you think. In a sales activity like the job-search process, it is always best to sell what the buyer wants to buy.

Do your homework before any interview. Obtain and review as much information as possible about the employer from the two primary research sources: published items (including information available on the Internet) and people. Research the organization using both sources; don't depend on just one. Talk to network contacts who might know something about the organization, the specific department or function, or the hiring manager. Other pre-interview homework might include

- reading annual and 10K reports for publicly traded companies,

- researching the organization in published directories and via computerized research tools,

- learning who the principal officers are,

- contacting the employer's advertising or public relations department/agency for information,

- reviewing product/service literature,

- checking the library for recent articles on the organization and its industry,

- reviewing company policies (if they are made available), and

- finding and reviewing the organization's Internet home page and any other relevant company or industry information available on-line.

Being able to mention salient facts about the potential employer will boost your confidence, help put you more at ease, show interviewers that you are interested in their organization, and possibly distinguish you from other candidates. With the wide variety of information easily accessible on the Internet, however, most hiring managers will expect that you have done your homework before the interview. You will probably stand out negatively if you have not prepared adequately.

Request the job description from the employer or from the search firm listing the position. Employers should be willing to share a job description with you if one exists. Analyze it to determine what you have that the organization needs, what you might be missing, and, most important, what value-added you might bring to the organization.

Recognize the employer's needs and how much it values the open position. Determine what types of applicants the company does not hire and what types it does. Some firms have a stated, or unstated, profile of desired candidates, and if your education, background, knowledge, skills, and experience deviate from the desired profile, you may have a hard time selling yourself.

Make a mental list of past projects and accomplishments and how they may apply to the organization and specific position you're seeking. Demonstrate how the employer would benefit by hiring you— how you can help the company solve its needs (particularly its immediate ones).

Custom-design each interview. Be prepared to ask questions to keep the conversation going, to obtain important information, to provide segues into detailing your accomplishments, and to show how your experience matches the employer's current or projected needs. An interview has a two-way agenda; the organization is interviewing you, but you are also interviewing it to determine if you want to work in this position and for this organization.

Develop a list of specific questions to ask the interviewer. Asking intelligent, focused questions about the company or the open position indicates that you are interested and have done your homework. Interviewers greatly prefer that you have a better response than "no" when they ask if you have any questions for them. Also develop questions to help determine problems that the organization and hiring manager are trying to solve, what qualifications they seek, if they have a preferred candidate profile, and, most important, whether you want the job if it is offered to you.

Bring extra copies of your résumé. Remember, however, that the organization selected you on the basis of the résumé it received, so it is not mandatory that you supply the interviewer with an updated version. If you think it will help your cause, you can always provide your updated résumé at the end of the interview or include it with your follow-up letter.

DURING AN INTERVIEW

Arriving

Don't arrive late; if you will be delayed, call before your scheduled appointment time. Offer to come in later or to reschedule if necessary. If you are going for an interview in a location you have never been before, consider taking a test drive (or the equivalent, if you use public transportation) one or two days before, not only to find out how to get there but also to detect any possible obstructions (for instance, road construction or detours).

Arrive ten minutes early at the least; earlier is even better. If you arrive very early, let the receptionist or security guard know that you are early and don't yet want to be announced. Use this pre-interview time to

- watch what goes on;
- observe the actions and attitudes of employees strolling through the lobby; and
- read any articles, wall postings, and company publications that might be available.

While waiting, try to note additional information about the organization, and also to get an in-person feel for the company and its culture. Your initial impressions are very important and usually on target. Don't let your growing enthusiasm as you continue through the interviewing process mask any major concerns or other issues that arose from your first impressions.

Make a pre-interview restroom stop. Make sure you look your best and that nothing is out of place.

Travel as lightly as possible. Many career counselors/outplacement consultants suggest not bringing your briefcase, but this is another "it depends" situation. At a minimum, carry a leather folder with a note pad and extra copies of your résumé and other supporting material.

At the Start

Use appropriate dress, a businesslike handshake, and direct eye contact to make a good first impression on the interviewer. A bad or weak first impression can be overcome, but doing so is very difficult.

Being properly dressed will not get you the job, but being poorly dressed, having a limp handshake, avoiding eye contact, and other negative aspects of your self-presentation can help you lose the opportunity. Determine the suggested dress beforehand (the human resources department or the company receptionist can be excellent sources of inquiry), but always dress a bit more conservatively than the situation might indicate. (Once there, it is usually easier to dress down than to dress up, particularly for men, who can just take off their coat or tie.)

Ask someone who will give you an objective opinion about the acceptability of your handshake. The range of acceptability is wide, but make sure your handshake is within that range (neither weak nor bone-crushing).

Because eye contact is so important, if normally you wear glasses, don't wear a pair that are tinted or have photogray or transition-type lenses. Interviewers need to be able to look into your eyes.

Act in a professional manner around everyone you meet. Assume that each person, from the receptionist or security personnel on, will have input into the hiring decision, so be on guard and exceedingly polite, even from the time you drive into the organization's parking lot (or exit the subway stop if it is near the employer's building). People from the organization may be looking out their window at the parking lot (or subway stop) and notice you and your actions.

Some interviewees seem to feel that they can mistreat or ignore the employer's administrative staff, then "turn it on" for the professionals who actually interview them. This misguided approach is one of the quickest ways to fail in the interviewing process. Any negative perceptions by support staff will be quickly reported back to the hiring manager and will likely doom your candidacy.

Sit in a straight-back chair (if given the option) rather than a soft chair or couch. But be sure the chair you choose is not the interviewer's preferred chair. Ask if you are unsure.

Reverify with each interviewer the time you will be spending with him or her, even if you had been provided a copy of the interview schedule. You may have planned what to say in the second half-hour of the interview but then need to make adjustments when you find out that you have only fifteen to twenty minutes with that interviewer instead of the scheduled hour.

Ask the interviewer if it is okay to take notes. On the rare occasion that the person says no, put away your pen and notebook.

Throughout

Convey a high level of energy and a sense of urgency. Show interviewers that your career and next position are very important to you. Be confident but not arrogant.

Sit up straight; avoid slouching or sitting back with your arms folded, even if the interviewer does. Hiring managers and other interviewers want candidates who generate energy and enthusiasm in their words, actions, and posture.

Get interviewers to like you. Hiring managers consistently admit that, once candidates have passed the initial screen and are in the interviewing stage, choosing one over another often boils down to the person's "likability." More than technical skills, experience, education, or career potential, making yourself liked influences the speed and outcome of the hiring process. Because your next boss probably will spend a lot of time with you, compatibility often is the key. Also, people who interview you and like you may be excellent network contacts for the remainder of your search. If you don't land the job or get selected for the next round of interviews, recontact these interviewers to ask for their help as you continue your search.

Don't bring up negative parts of your work history, skills, background, or education. As with your résumé, emphasize the positive and omit or downplay any negatives. Always be ready, however, to address negatives if they come up.

Avoid criticizing former employers, bosses, colleagues, or direct reports. You never know who knows (or is related to) whom. Also, interviewers don't want to listen to complainers; they might think you would do the same about them if they hire you. As emphasized in Chapter 1, your goal in the job search is to put the past behind you.

Be an active listener. Doing so will give you a better chance to determine the needs of the hiring manager and the organization and perhaps how to best sell yourself to meet those needs. Often interviewers provide hints to which you can tailor your subsequent responses. By listening carefully, you also will be better able to determine if you want to work for the organization if offered the position.

Discuss what you can *do and would like to do, not what you cannot and will not do.* Focus on your skills, strengths, accomplishments, and the short- and long-term contributions you can make to the organization and to the hiring manager.

Ask why the position is open and what happened to the incumbent, if there was one. Finding out if the position is a new one, if the person formerly in it was promoted (or fired), if five people have held the position in the past two years, or if the hiring manager was the incumbent (or has held the open position in the past) can help you decide how to approach the opportunity or whether you want the job.

Be prepared to defend your résumé. Don't assume that interviewers will understand or accept your résumé just because it looks good, you worked very hard on it, and it goes well beyond "good enough" in your opinion and the opinions of any résumé editors/reviewers who have read it.

Be ready for interviewers who have a copy of your résumé but obviously have not read it. You are now meeting with them, so your résumé has done its primary job. Don't act annoyed that the interviewer has not read your résumé (or, even worse, remind him or her of that fact). Forget about the document: You are now face to face with the interviewer and have his or her attention, so tell your story.

Present the important points you want to make as soon as is reasonably possible. If you wait until the end of the interview, you may not get the opportunity.

Try not to answer more than you are asked. Say what you need to and then stop. In most cases, talk for no more than one to two minutes at a time. If you do go longer on occasion, pause and ask the interviewer if you are responding appropriately (answering the question asked), so that he or she can redirect you if necessary.

Don't rescind a reply, even if it is followed by a long pause or disappointing body language from the interviewer. If you need to make any corrections, do so when your responses to subsequent questions provide the opportunity.

If asked what seems like a trick or particularly tough question, consider saying, "That's an interesting ***question; let me think about it for a while."*** Then take ten to twenty seconds to compose yourself and prepare a response. Do not use the word *interesting* in this way too often in the same interview, or the interviewer will figure out what you are doing.

Don't be afraid of silence. Periods of silence occasionally occur in interviews. Have a few questions ready so that, if the silence becomes extended, you can jump in with a question, but try not to fill every silent period. The interviewer may need time to ponder your responses or come up with the next question. Also, after giving your response to a question, wait; it is now the interviewer's turn to ask for clarification, raise another question, or perhaps comment on your response.

Don't be surprised to find yourself answering the same questions multiple times. This situation can occur either as you meet with multiple interviewers or when you come back for multiple rounds with the same interviewer. In the latter case, don't assume that the interviewer will have remembered what you previously said, but ask when in doubt.

Save* your *tougher questions until later in the interview. Hold potentially sensitive queries until everyone has relaxed and you sense that the interviewer likes you.

Don't act annoyed if the interview is interrupted. Simply resume the conversation by summarizing what just had been said, and then continue. If the interview is interrupted several times, take that as a possible indication of the organization's culture or the working style of the interviewer.

Broach the subject of overqualification if you think it may be an issue, but be cautious about bringing it up; that is, don't make it an issue. Rather than arguing that you are not overqualified, point out the advantages of your experience. Stress your ability to solve the organization's problems quickly because of your extensive experience.

Near the End

Express your interest and enthusiasm for the position and organization, but only if you are interested. Be explicit: Don't assume that interviewers will know you are interested simply because you went through the interviewing process with them.

Consider asking, "If I were a spectacular success in this position after six months (or a year), what would I have accomplished?" The interviewer's response will give you some idea of his or her real (or unreal) expectations for the position and the person to be hired. Then you can judge if these expectations are realistic, and how easy (or impossible) it would be for you to achieve them.

Be prepared to summarize why you are a good candidate. You might do this in response to an interviewer's question or consider bringing it up yourself to help "close the sale." Leave each of the interviewers, particularly the hiring manager, with the impression that you have heard and understood the organization's needs and that you are the best person to address and fulfill these needs.

Near the end of an interview that you think went well, or for a position you are very interested in, consider asking the following three questions:

1. *What will be the process from this point?* This question can be put in a variety of ways, but try to get a sense of how many candidates are being considered, how many will be brought back for the next round (if there is to be a next round), who will be the interviewer(s) in the next round and subsequent rounds, how many rounds there will there be, when a decision will be made on whatever the next step(s) will be, and when an offer is expected to be made.

2. *Why do you think I'm a good candidate for the position?* This question is similar in purpose to "Why did you select me?" suggested earlier

to ask when you are invited for an interview. Again, in a sales activity such as the job search, you want to emphasize what the buyer wants to buy rather than a random set of things you have to offer, no matter how impressive those random things may seem to be.

3. *What concerns do you have about me as a candidate?* The goal here is to identify and correct any misconceptions immediately and, if you cannot, to at least get a sense of where you stand. Of course, you might think of a response or clarification regarding an area of concern on the way home, after the tension of the interview has dissipated. If the response is important enough, call (or e-mail) the interviewer as soon as possible; otherwise, include the response or clarification in your follow-up letter.

Ask Question 1 of every interviewer, and note discrepancies between interviewers. Remember that any information you receive in response can put you ahead, but also that anything interviewers say about the remainder of the interviewing process is subject to change—even if they believe what they say, are trying to be honest with you, and have the best intentions.

You don't have to use the exact wording of these questions, but ask similar questions to elicit what they aim to obtain. Not all interviewers will answer these questions, and some might react negatively to Questions 2 and 3, but asking them is worth a try. Because the job search is a sales and marketing effort, posing these questions helps you think about closing the sale.

If the employer is clearly interested in you, ask to meet more organization members. These additional meetings might be held while you are there or during a subsequent visit or visits. Many job offers are made after only two interviews—with a human resources representative and the hiring manager. You owe it to yourself to get more information about the position and the organization, and to meet with more people. Remember that you are evaluating the employer as well as it evaluating you. Ask to spend time with others, particularly your would-be peers, any direct reports, the hiring manager's boss, and possibly others higher up in the organization (but be reasonable about your demands and expectations here).

Be yourself and try to have fun. View an interview as an opportunity, not an inquisition, and the position as one you can, and want to, walk away from if it is not the right situation for you.

THE FOLLOW-UP

How you follow up after each interview can be critically important to your success.

Immediately after each interview or set of interviews, handwrite or type up a set of notes; even better, tape-record your observations, thoughts, and impressions. You can do this with an easily transportable microcassette recorder, ideally as soon as possible to capture those extremely valuable first impressions. Save the tape to prepare the near-mandatory follow-up thank-you letter, and also for review if you are selected for the next round of interviews.

Evaluate what went well and what could be improved. Concentrate on what you will do differently the next time you interview with that firm or others; don't be too hard on yourself for mistakes you think you made. You might never find out what happened and how you really did. (For instance, there could have been a preselected internal candidate, and the interviewers were just "going through the motions" with you.)

Send a follow-up letter to everyone you spent time with. This less-than-a-page and preferably typed letter should be sent within twenty-four hours. You should send a different (or at least somewhat different) version to each interviewer you met with in case all your letters end up in the same folder on the hiring manager's desk. Faxing or e-mailing this letter can reduce the receipt time and is a widely accepted practice, although some interviewers may consider it too casual. If you e-mail your response, send it as quickly as possible; an e-mail follow-up received two or three days after the fact will seem like an eternity in Internet time.

In your follow-up letter(s)

- thank the interviewer(s) for their time and interest;

- review the interview highlights, including your statement of why the organization should hire you (if appropriate), and express your continuing interest in the possibilities that were discussed; and

- be sincere and direct in your tone.

In the past, interviewees may have distinguished themselves from other candidates by sending these post-interview thank-you letters; now you may stand out if you don't send them.

Follow up by phone if you have not heard from the employer's representative by the time he or she set. This is one reason you try to get a response to the "What's the (rest of the) process?" question near the end of each interview.

Don't badger the hiring manager or others in the organization. And don't expect things to move along faster than an interviewer indicated they would. Unforeseen delays will probably creep into the hiring process; they almost always do.

IF YOU DON'T GET THE OFFER (OR GET INVITED BACK)

Ask for feedback. Get back to the interviewer(s), particularly any you felt you made a connection with, to ask why. Tell them that, because you are still in the job market, you would appreciate their input so that you can do better when interviewing with the next organization. Some will be willing to help you, and some won't. And even though some of those who seem willing won't be entirely open about why you did not land the position, or won't actually cite any shortcomings in your interviewing techniques or personal mannerisms, it is still worth asking. Do not try to use this opportunity, however, to attempt to convince the interviewer that the organization made a mistake by not selecting you.

Try to find out who was hired for the position, and contact and congratulate that person. In talking with him or her, you might discover some new leads for your job search. If the person agrees to meet with you, it is probably better to do so off-site, perhaps for breakfast or lunch, to avoid a potentially awkward situation for the hiring organization or manager.

9

Persevering in the Job Search

F OR MOST JOB SEEKERS, the search process is more like a marathon than a sprint, and one run over a hilly course. Be prepared for the peaks and valleys. This chapter suggests ways to keep motivated in the intellectually and emotionally challenging job-search process, particularly if you lost your previous job.

CHECKING YOUR PROGRESS

Find a "job-search buddy." Team up with a friend or network contact and meet at least once a week to share ideas, problems, advice, opportunities, and specific search plans for the coming week.

Do an overall analysis of your search—ideally with someone else— on a regular basis, perhaps monthly or bimonthly. Review your activities, activity level, and results; then decide if you need to adjust your strategy or tactics or increase your activity level. Although you could do this status check yourself or enlist a trusted friend for the review, consider getting objective help from a career counselor or outplacement consultant.

STAYING MOTIVATED

When Out of Work

Dress as if for work each morning. It is a good way to start your job-search day positively.

Leave the house at least once a day to make contact with the outside world. It is very easy to feel, and become, isolated when out of work.

Find others who are or have been out of work and get their support. Employed veterans of previous unemployment—people who are positive and were not embittered by the experience—can be extremely supportive and helpful to those currently out of work. Seek out these individuals and ask for their assistance.

Do volunteer work. Donate your time, talents, and energy to organizations and activities that interest you and could benefit from your professional skills. Volunteering will keep you active, productive, and focused, and it may even add something to your résumé. Being involved also may increase your network of contacts: You never know who knows, or is related to, someone who might be of help in your search. Make sure, however, that volunteer work does not consume your time. The proper balance of job-search and volunteer time ultimately rests with the individual.

Try to keep your life balanced in ways unrelated to your search. Although the job search for those out of work should be a full-time effort (whatever that means for you), the emotional and intellectual demands of the process can lead to burn-out. Schedule in some downtime; it helps renew creativity, health, and energy.

Don't succumb to the "yeah, but . . . " syndrome. A common condition afflicting job seekers, particularly those out of work who have been looking for a while, is the response "yeah, but . . . " to people's suggestions ("I can't, or won't, do that because . . . "). This condition can be extremely detrimental to your search; if those trying to help hear your "yeah, but . . . " more than a few times, they probably will stop making suggestions.

Whether or Not Currently Employed

Set reasonable goals, but approach your job search one day at a time. You can easily overdo it by taking on too many tasks at once.

Spend time each week helping other job seekers. You will probably get back a lot more than you give.

Participate in job-search support groups to help counterbalance any sense of isolation. Sharing stories about your successes and failures and encouraging fellow job seekers can make the search process more tolerable, and maybe even fun.

Be proactive but patient. Once you have mastered the skills and your job-search campaign is under way, it is a matter of numbers. If you keep your activity level high you are bound to succeed. Remember that attitude and activity are perhaps the two most important personal factors in the job search and the primary things you, as a job seeker, have some control over.

THE EMOTIONAL SIDE REVISITED

Prepare for rejections; they are a normal part of the search process. You are likely to experience a number of rejections before you find a job; consider them part of the indignities of the job-search process.

Try not to get too discouraged. The job search is an art, not a science. There are no formulas, no guarantees. If you work hard and intelligently at the process while staying focused and positive, however, you eventually will be successful. Keep reviewing your accomplishments (and your PAR/STAR statements as discussed in Chapter 3) to remind yourself that you were a valuable asset to an organization before and will be so again.

Avoid negative or bitter people who sometimes can drag you down with them. Venting your feelings with others is fine, but it is probably counterproductive if the venting sessions go on too long or if they occur too frequently. It can be very difficult if your spouse/significant other/partner fits into this category of negative or bitter people. Get professional help, and other support, if you find your-self in this situation.

Work at managing the inevitable emotional ups and downs of the job-search process. Emotional peaks and valleys are a normal reaction to the situation, whether or not you are employed, and the ups and downs often feel more pronounced when you are out of work.

When you get good news and are excited, use this positive ener-gy to generate more job-search activity. Make more phone calls, write more letters, and send more e-mail messages; even better, concentrate your efforts on doing whatever is the hardest for you in your search. These energy boosts can make you up to three or four times more pro-ductive and also will help you come across as more confident and competent.

Learn stress-reduction techniques and get professional help when you need it. Stress is a natural part of the job-search process; learn how to deal with it effectively so that it does not paralyze you.

Make sure that something is always in the pipeline. Just because a lead is promising or an offer seems imminent, do not suspend your other search efforts. If this lead or offer falls through, your other work should result in more job possibilities. Keep focused on moving for-ward in your search.

Watch for personal warning signs that indicate you need a break to compose yourself. Your temper can shorten when you are unem-ployed, frustrated, and worried. But even when looking for a job while employed, there may be times when you need to stop or slow down the process for a while to regroup.

Take a break at least once a week. Go for a long walk, see a movie, go fishing—do something you like to do. Get away from the tele-phone, the mailbox, and your computer. Set manageable goals, do your best to accomplish them, and then reward yourself with a break.

10

Negotiating Job Offers

THEY WANT YOU; you are about to get a job offer. Congratulations again! This can be a time of great joy and hopefulness when you, as a job seeker, feel excited, accomplished, and successful. Unfortunately, it can often be a time of near panic as well, because many job seekers have little experience negotiating job offers. If job-search skills are not often used, then negotiating skills are called upon even less frequently.

This chapter tells you how to prepare for negotiations and gives you some ideas for the face-to-face negotiation session. It also addresses what you should do after accepting or rejecting an offer and points out a few things to keep in mind before and after starting your new position.

PREPARING FOR NEGOTIATION

Research the typical salary or salary range for the position(s) you are going after. A critically important, but often overlooked, part of the job-search process is developing a realistic view of what the current marketplace is paying for positions requiring your knowledge, skills, experience, and education.

The best way to get salary information is through *networking*. Although it is socially unacceptable to ask all but your closest friends their actual salary, asking the salary range for target positions in friends' or network contacts' organizations is fine; they will probably tell you if they know and if their firms commonly share such information.

Other excellent sources for salary information are *agencies and search firms*, particularly those focusing on your discipline or industry. Search professionals are market brokers on a nearly constant basis, and they know what the market rate is for certain positions in certain industries and geographical areas. Getting their attention so that they will share this valuable information with you, however, can be difficult if you don't fit the specific candidate criteria for the search(es) they are currently conducting.

Local chapters of *professional associations* in your field may have job referral services, and the people who run these member services (usually volunteers) could be another good source.

Published salary surveys also are available from the government, in trade journals, and on the Internet, although some may be outdated, or too general, to be useful.

Try to develop a realistic range for what is being paid in the marketplace. The range could be quite wide, and of course some firms will pay over it and others will pay under it, but your confidence will rise when you know the normal range to expect.

Remember that your current, or previous, salary is not the best determinant of what you will be paid in your next job. Certainly, when we move to a new employer we would all like to receive a 10 to 20 percent increase (along with stock options and a sign-on bonus), but such an increase (or package) is not guaranteed, no matter how good the job market is. Again, the critical factor is what is being paid in the marketplace for positions requiring your knowledge, skills, experience, and education.

Determine the rock-bottom salary you will accept long before you get to the offer stage. This figure should be the absolute minimum you could afford to, or would want to, accept for a job that is ideal in every other way. Determining this figure does not mean that you will have to settle for it.

Avoid mentioning salary first. The basic rule throughout the job-search process, and particularly during interviewing and negotiating, is that he or she who mentions salary first loses. If possible, get the employer interested in you before compensation issues are discussed.

Treat an offer you are about to receive as a confirmation of your skills and marketplace value—and also as a stimulus to pursue additional opportunities. Recontact other employers who have expressed interest in you to let them know you are about to receive an offer. Perhaps you can force a decision from one of them, giving you two (or more) offers from which to choose. Trying to get something else going is not being disloyal to a potential employer but is self-protection; it is not unusual for even the most promising opportunity to be put on hold, or to evaporate, for a variety of reasons, often having nothing to do with the candidate.

Consider each opportunity for the professional development it will provide, in addition to the salary and benefits it offers. A key ongoing career concern should be your "employability"—this has replaced the concept of job security. Ask yourself how this opportunity will position you for the future. Will it give you the technical, professional, and managerial experience you'll need to move into your more ideal job? Will it give you access to people (such as co-workers and clients) who could become excellent contacts for your future career?

Try to understand the employer's position. Look at the situation objectively, or at least as objectively as you can. Recognize a potential employer's need to balance risk (its hope, not guarantee, of what you can accomplish for it) and reward (what it is willing to offer up front, before you have started and your level of contribution is established).

Link your negotiation goals to the employer's goals. If what you feel is appropriate exceeds the employer's limits (what the organization is willing to give or capable of giving), you must either modify your goal(s) or decline the offer.

Get the offer before you discuss the specific employment terms in detail. Although you can position yourself through your actions in approaching the organization and during the interviewing process, the real negotiation process starts when the organization is interested enough to make you an offer.

Express your appreciation when the offer is extended, and reinforce your interest in the position. Don't accept on the spot, however.

Ask for the offer in writing. Verbal offers are great to receive, but always ask for written confirmation. If nothing else, the wait for the written offer will buy you time to consider it, while you evaluate the status of any other of your job prospects.

Don't assume that you must negotiate every offer (or every aspect of every offer). Negotiate only if the offer is not acceptable.

THE NEGOTIATING SESSION

Request a meeting for formal negotiations. Set up a face-to-face meeting unless geographical or economic restrictions make it impossible or unrealistic.

Be thoroughly prepared, believe in yourself, and be clear about your priorities and areas of compromise. Throughout the negotiating process, realize that both sides have something at stake, and that reaching a win-win agreement is just as important for the employer as it is for you. After all, the conclusion of negotiations will, you hope, mark the beginning of a satisfying and mutually beneficial employer-employee relationship.

Continually try to preserve your relationship with the organization and hiring manager during the negotiation process. Mention how pleased you are about the offer first and use positive statements throughout the session.

Try to depersonalize the negotiations. Although it may feel like your career and life are hanging in the balance, treat each negotiating session as a business meeting being held to resolve a set of business issues.

Set out all the areas you want to negotiate at the beginning of the session. Otherwise you might create the suspicion that there will always be one more item about to be disclosed, and the hiring manager or employer representative may be unwilling to make concessions on any issue.

Be prepared to justify your desired compensation when the money topic arises. Use logical and objective reasoning; an emotional appeal is not as effective. The research you have done on current salary ranges will prove beneficial here. This is the time to mention other offers you might have, but do not fabricate any as a negotiating tactic.

If you think the salary offer is low but you are still interested, try to negotiate an earlier salary review. Propose to have your first formal performance/salary review at three or six months, versus a year. Use this tactic, however, only if you are sure that (1) you can prove your worth to the organization quickly, and (2) the hiring manager has or can get the approval for this early review/increase. You might ask for a signing bonus, although such bonuses are not typically given by most firms.

Get the final agreement in writing. You can do so by getting the employer to generate an amended offer letter for you to sign, or by writing a letter documenting the discussions and final resolutions and sending it to the hiring manager/organization as a referenced attachment to your signed offer letter. The former approach is preferable.

AFTER ACCEPTING OR REJECTING AN OFFER

Contact your references as soon as possible after accepting a new position (or rejecting an offer). Thank them for their help. If you declined an offer, explain why, so that they will be willing to help when your next job opportunity arises.

Call or send a short note to other network contacts to let them know of your successful transition and to thank them. Some job seekers send these announcements after they get business cards from their new organization, but why wait? There is no harm in sending one letter soon after you accept the position and a second—perhaps on your new company's stationery—once your new business cards arrive.

Do not use your old company's stationery for any announcement letter that you send after accepting the position. And don't forget my "Dear Sandy" story from Chapter 4.

While not aggressively seeking new opportunities before starting your new job, be willing to talk about other employment possibilities. If you get a call from an employer you had communicated with previously, be willing to talk with that organization's representative, and even to interview, if it seems like a good opportunity. Even after you have accepted a written offer and set a start date, the hiring organization could renege before that date for a variety of reasons—probably none of them having nothing to do with you. Therefore, considering other opportunities is not treasonous, just self-defensive.

If you get a subsequent offer that you would prefer to take, inform the first firm of the situation and explain that you *will* follow through with the commitment you have already made but that you have received a second offer that is of great interest to you. (Cite the specific reasons.) In many but unfortunately not all cases, the first firm will release you from your commitment, realizing that you could begin looking for another position soon after you started working for it.

When turning down a position, write a letter rejecting the offer, or confirming your rejection of it if you have already let the organization or hiring manager know by phone. Be careful to retain as positive a relationship as possible with the hiring organization and its representatives: You may be a candidate some time in the future, or you may approach it later for some other business purpose.

STARTING A NEW POSITION

Before starting your new position, prepare your new manager for any inevitable mistake(s). These are particularly likely to occur if you worked at your previous organization a long time. These mistakes often are cultural errors, but their significance can be great.

It is not unusual to make an error in the first few months at a new organization, and when you ask why you were not told or cautioned about this situation, being told that it is "something everyone knows." You have just stepped on a cultural land mine by doing something that might have been completely acceptable at your old organization. Talk to your new manager ahead of time about this possibility; ask for his or her help in avoiding these potential, but unfortunately common, disasters.

Update your résumé during the first week in your new position. Particularly if you lost your previous job, you have learned the hard way that there is no such thing as job security. Always be ready for management changes, hostile takeovers, poor quarterly results, and other factors that might negatively affect your job status. In those situations, the last one in—in this case you—is often the first one out. By updating your résumé, you are not being disloyal to your new employer; you are just being wise about your career. Keeping your résumé current is also a first, but important, intellectual and emotional step in maintaining your employability.

Help those who come after you. By now you will have learned the value of networking in the job search and received help from a number of people, some of whom probably were near strangers at the start of the process. Be prepared to return the favor by helping others with their searches. Be very willing to give field research meetings/informational interviews to job seekers and career changers who contact you. If you are too busy in your new position to meet them at your office during work hours, suggest getting together for breakfast or after work. (And, now that you are re-employed, plan to pick up the tab.)

Maintain your personal network. Building and expanding your network while searching for a job is critical, but maintaining it is just as important—and can be even more difficult when you get busy with the responsibilities of your new position. Make an effort to maintain and enhance your network as a key aspect of ensuring your employability.

11

Final Job-Search Tips

OVERALL CONSIDERATIONS

Think "it depends" first when considering any answer to a job-search question. As noted throughout this book, "it depends" is the only answer to most of these questions. Decide when and how (or if) you will add any new concept, technique, or approach to your search repertoire. But keep in mind that there are no magic bullets in the job search.

Become a student of the process. Learn and implement effective job-search methods, and build and reinforce a personal network to help you now and in the future.

Avoid taking the easy way out in any of your job-search activities. If you really want to find a job—and the "right" job for you—limit the number of times you intentionally cut corners.

TO START THE PROCESS

Select your references carefully and early; make finalizing them one of your first job-search tasks. Your references are very important to your job search, so don't subject them to annoying calls, be sure to nurture them, and keep them informed of your search progress.

Make it easy for people to contact you. Here are two simple but very effective ways:

- Use your résumé header as the letterhead for your reference list and letters related to your job search. This approach will help to give your written material a polished and consistent look and will display your phone number (and possibly e-mail address) prominently on all your correspondence.

- Have personal business cards printed, particularly if you are out of work.

Finish your résumé and then move on. As stated in Chapter 3, the "perfect résumé" is just a myth. You want one "good enough" to help get you interviews. Work hard to produce a résumé that you are proud of and then concentrate on the more difficult aspects of job search—primarily networking.

THROUGHOUT THE PROCESS

Use your résumé to get you in the door and to prepare you for interviewing. Don't expect your résumé to do anything more than these primary functions.

Keep in mind the two primary steps in the job search: getting interviews and then getting job offers. Having a great résumé won't get you hired but might win you the opportunity to tell an interviewer your story.

Inform your references each time you plan to use them. They should know the kind of job for which you are being considered and how you have presented yourself to the potential employer. Be sure to contact them again a few days later to find out whether they were called for a reference check and, if so, how they thought the conversation went.

Plan for a lengthy search but hope for (and work toward) a short one. Building momentum in the job search usually takes time, but, as with most things in life, timing is everything.

Don't be concerned about competition for a specific job or competition in general. You cannot do anything about the competition, so focus on the positive things you can offer an employer.

Believe in yourself. Being self-confident but not cocky will help convey an image of your overall competence. It takes a lot of inner strength to be successful in the intellectually and emotionally demanding job-search process, but if you work hard and persevere, you can do it.

Plan your work and then work your plan. Stick to a daily and weekly schedule but be flexible so that you will always be able to recognize and seize opportunities you had not anticipated.

Take an active role in your search. You can create opportunities for yourself by (1) clearly articulating your skills, experience, and accomplishments; (2) learning the needs of potential employers; (3) communicating with as many people as possible; and (4) being flexible, enthusiastic, and politely persistent.

Research the typical salary (or salary range) for the position(s) you are going after. It is critically important to establish a realistic view of what the current marketplace is paying for positions requiring your knowledge, skills, experience, and education.

Avoid mentioning salary first. Remember that throughout the job-search process, and particularly during interviewing and negotiating, he or she who mentions salary first loses. Get the employer interested in you before discussing compensation issues.

Recognize that, besides the amount and quality of your search efforts, other factors can affect the length of the process:

- Your attitude

- The condition of the job market

- The job type and salary level you want

- Geographical limitations or preferences

- Factors beyond your control (for instance, age or other types of discrimination)

- Timing

- Luck

Identify, develop, and implement parallel or backup job-search goals and strategies. Or at least be on the lookout for these possibilities.

Although focus is critical in the job search, concentrating all your efforts in one area may be emotionally devastating if you have little or no success.

Be polite and persistent in your networking and other job-search efforts. *Politeness* means being nice to people, remembering their names, and sending appropriate thank-you notes in a timely manner. *Persistence* is required because employers' attention can be diverted, and your interest in an open position will almost always be more intense than the employer's desire to fill it, despite what the employer may claim.

Determine the needs of hiring organizations and specific hiring managers. Research prospective employers in general and specific companies to learn their concerns.

Look at each opportunity for the professional development it will provide. Professional development is important to maintaining your employability, and employability has replaced the concept of job security in today's marketplace.

Try to hear what your search is telling you. What is and is not working? Do you need to increase your activity level, extend your focus area(s), change directions, get professional help for job-search concerns or emotional issues?

Maintain and track your search activity level. You can measure progress by counting the number of phone calls you make or e-mail messages you send daily, letters you send weekly, networking/field research meetings you have weekly, and interviews you have monthly. Set numeric goals in each category. Regularly review your progress toward these goals and adapt your strategies and tactics where necessary.

HANGING IN THERE

Don't get too discouraged. If you work hard and intelligently at the process while staying focused and positive, you eventually will be successful. Remind yourself what you have accomplished in your past work and how much of an asset you will be to your next employer.

Try to manage the emotional highs and lows that are inevitable in the search process. Deal with the lows as best you can, and when you get good news and are excited, use this positive energy to generate more job-search activity. Make more phone calls, write more letters, and send more e-mail messages; use this boost to concentrate your efforts on doing whatever is hardest for you in your search.

Beware of the "yeah, but . . ." syndrome. If you keep making excuses to people who are offering you help, they are likely to stop doing so.

Be sure to keep job leads coming through the pipeline. Just because one lead seems very promising, or even if an offer is near, don't stop your other search efforts. If this lead or offer falls through, your other work will provide you with more job options and prevent you from falling into a depression.

Regularly do an analysis of your search, perhaps monthly or bimonthly. Look at your activities, activity level, and results and then decide if you need to adjust your strategy in any of these areas.

Remember that if you are currently out of work, you are not alone. Many others have been unemployed, particularly in the tumultuous 1990s; most have survived and even thrived. Try to view this setback as a temporary condition to turn into an opportunity.

Stay active, stay focused, stay motivated: You will succeed. Getting a job is challenging work. Remember to apply the old Nike marketing slogan to your search efforts: "Just Do It!" But "do it" thoughtfully and well, generally following the advice given in this book—tempered, of course, by "it depends."

Good luck in your search!

Selected Bibliography

THE FOLLOWING PUBLICATIONS and Web sites are grouped by topic, starting with the job search in general; the sections follow the order in which the topics are presented in this book. Based on their content, some books have been listed multiple times.

Overall Job Search

Bolles, Richard Nelson. *What Color Is Your Parachute?* Berkeley, Calif.: Ten Speed Press, republished annually.

Burton, Mary Lindley, and Richard A. Wedemeyer. *In Transition*. New York: Harper Business, 1991.

Dawson, Kenneth, and Sheryl Dawson. *Job Search: The Total System*. 2d ed. New York: Wiley, 1996.

Hakim, Cliff. *When You Lose Your Job*. San Francisco: Berrett-Kohler, 1993.

Knox, Deborah H., and Sandra S. Butzel. *Life Work Transitions.com: Putting Your Spirit Online*. Boston: Butterworth-Heinemann, 2000.

Lucht, John. *Executive Job-Changing Workbook*. New York: Viceroy, 1994.

———. *The New Rules of Passage at $100,000+: The Insider's Lifetime Guide to Executive Job-Changing and Faster Career Progress*. Rev. ed. New York: Viceroy, 1999.

Yate, Martin. *Knock 'Em Dead*. Holbrook, Mass.: Adams, republished annually.

The Emotional Side

Bridges, William. *Transitions: Making Sense of Life's Changes*. Reading, Mass.: Perseus Books, 1980.

Hakim, Cliff. *When You Lose Your Job*. San Francisco: Berrett-Kohler, 1993.

Self-Assessment and Career Change

Bolles, Richard Nelson. *What Color Is Your Parachute?* Berkeley, Calif.: Ten Speed Press, republished annually.

Burton, Mary Lindley, and Richard A. Wedemeyer. *In Transition*. New York: Harper Business, 1991.

Butler, Timothy, and James Waldroop. *Discovering Your Career in Business*. Reading, Mass.: Perseus Books, 1997.

Everett, Melissa. *Making a Living While Making a Difference: A Guide to Creating Careers with a Conscience*. New York: Bantam, 1995.

Gilman, Cheryl. *Doing the Work You Love: Discovering Your Purpose and Realizing Your Dreams*. Chicago: Contemporary, 1997.

Hirsch, Arlene S. *Love Your Work and Success Will Follow*. New York: Wiley, 1996.

Knox, Deborah H., and Sandra S. Butzel. *Life Work Transitions.com: Putting Your Spirit Online*. Boston: Butterworth-Heinemann, 2000.

Kroeger, Otto, and Janet Thuesen. *Type Talk at Work*. New York: Dell, 1992.

Kummerov, Jean M.; Nancy J. Barger; and Linda K. Kirby. *Work Types*. New York: Warner, 1997.

Sher, Barbara. *It's Only Too Late If You Don't Start Now: How to Create Your Second Life at Any Age*. New York: Dell, 1999.

———. *Live the Life You Love*. New York: Dell, 1996.

———, with Anne Gottlieb. *Wishcraft: How to Get What You Really Want*. New York: Ballantine, 1979.

———, with Barbara Smith. *I Could Do Anything If I Only Knew What It Was: How to Discover What You Really Want and How to Get It*. New York: Dell, 1994.

Sinetar, Marsha. *Do What You Love, the Money Will Follow*. New York: Dell, 1987.

———. *To Build the Life You Want, Create the Work You Love*. New York: St. Martin's, 1995.

Tieger, Paul D., and Barbara Barron-Tieger. *Do What You Are: Discover the Perfect Career for You Through the Secrets of Personality Type*. 2d ed. Boston: Little Brown, 1995.

Also see the Web sites <www.careerdiscovery.com> and <www.futurestep.com>.

Financial Considerations

Beyer, Cathy; Doris Pike; and Loretta McGovern. *Surviving Unemployment*. New York: Henry Holt, 1993.

Dominguez, Joe, and Vicki Robin. *Your Money or Your Life: Transforming Your Relationship with Money and Achieving Financial Independence*. New York: Penguin, 1992.

Pond, Jonathan D. *1001 Ways to Cut Your Expenses*. New York: Dell, 1992.

Stanley, Thomas J., and William D. Danko. *The Millionaire Next Door: The Surprising Secrets of America's Wealthy*. New York: Pocket Books, 1996.

Résumés

Besson, Taunee. *National Business Employment Weekly Guide to Resumes*. 3d ed. New York: Wiley, 1999.

Yate, Martin. *Résumés That Knock 'Em Dead*. 3d ed. Holbrook, Mass.: Adams, 1998.

Job-Search Letters

Beatty, Richard H. *175 High-Impact Cover Letters*. 2d ed. Holbrook, Mass.: Adams, 1996.

————. *The Perfect Cover Letter*. 2d ed. Holbrook, Mass.: Adams, 1997.

Besson, Taunee. *National Business Employment Weekly: Cover Letters*. 3d ed. New York: Wiley, 1999.

Frank, William S. *200 Letters for Job Hunters*. Rev. ed. Berkeley, Calif.: Ten Speed Press, 1993.

Yate, Martin. *Cover Letters That Knock 'Em Dead*. 3d ed. Holbrook, Mass.: Adams, 1998.

Research

Bolles, Richard Nelson. *Job-Hunting on the Internet*. 2d ed. Berkeley, Calif.: Ten Speed Press, 1999.

Crowther, Karmen N. T. *Researching Your Way to a Good Job*. New York: Wiley, 1993.

Knox, Deborah H., and Sandra S. Butzel. *Life Work Transitions.com: Putting Your Spirit Online*. Boston: Butterworth-Heinemann, 2000.

Levine, Jeffrey P. *Doing Business in Boston*. 3d ed. Boston: Boston Business Journal, 1998.

Networking

Beatty, Richard H. *Richard Beatty's Job Search Networking*. Holbrook, Mass.: Adams, 1994.

Fisher, Donna, and Sandy Vilas. *Power Networking: 55 Secrets for Personal and Professional Success*. Austin, Tex.: Bard, 1992.

Kerr, Cherie. *Networking Skills That Will Get You the Job You Want*. Cincinnati, Ohio: Betterway, 1999.

Mackay, Harvey. *Dig Your Well before You're Thirsty*. New York: Currency Doubleday, 1997.

Richardson, Douglas B. *National Business Employment Weekly: Networking*. New York: Wiley, 1994.

RoAne, Susan. *The Secrets of Savvy Networking*. New York: Warner, 1993.

Tullier, L. Michele. *Networking for Everyone: Connecting with People for Career and Job Success*. Indianapolis: JIST Works, 1998.

Search Firms

Hunt, Christopher H., and Scott A. Scanlon. *Job Seekers' Guide to Executive Recruiters*. New York: Wiley, 1997.

———. *Job Seekers' Guide to Silicon Valley Recruiters*. New York: Wiley, 1998.

———. *Job Seekers' Guide to Wall Street Recruiters*. New York: Wiley, 1998.

Kennedy Information. *International Directory of Executive Recruiters*. 5th ed. Fitzwilliam, N.H.: Kennedy Information, 1998.

———. *Kennedy's Pocket Guide to Working with Executive Recruiters*. Rev. ed. Fitzwilliam, N.H.: Kennedy Information, 1996.

———. *The Directory of Executive Recruiters*. Fitzwilliam, N.H.: Kennedy Information, republished annually.

———. *The Directory of Temporary Placement Firms for Executives, Managers, and Professionals*. 9th ed. Fitzwilliam, N.H.: Kennedy Information, 1999.

Lucht, John. *The New Rules of Passage at $100,000+: The Insider's Lifetime Guide to Executive Job-Changing and Faster Career Progress*. Rev. ed. New York: Viceroy, 1998.

Sibbald, John. *The New Career Makers*. Rev. ed. New York: Harper Business, 1995.

Responding to Ads

See the Web site <www.nationaladsearch.com>.

Interviewing

Allen, Jeffrey G. *The Complete Q & A Job Interview Book*. 2d ed. New York: Wiley, 1997.

Beatty, Richard H. *The Five-Minute Interview*. 2d ed. New York: Wiley, 1998.

Drake, John D. *The Perfect Interview: How To Get the Job You Really Want*. 2d ed. New York: Amacom, 1997.

Hirsch, Arlene S. *National Business Employment Weekly: Interviewing*. 3d ed. New York: Wiley, 1999.

Medley, H. Anthony. *Sweaty Palms: The Neglected Art of Interviewing*. Rev. ed. Berkeley, Calif.: Ten Speed Press, 1993.

Yate, Martin. *Knock 'Em Dead*. Holbrook, Mass.: Adams, republished annually.

Related Topics

Hakim, Cliff. *We Are All Self-Employed: The New Social Contract for Working in a Changed World*. San Francisco: Berrett-Kohler, 1994.

Thrailkill, Diane. *Executive Temp*. New York: Random House, 1999.

Woods, Saralee Terry. *Executive Temping: A Guide for Professionals*. New York: Wiley, 1998.

Index

About the Author

ROBERT S. GARDELLA is the Assistant Director of Alumni Career Services at the Harvard Business School. He has worked as a consultant, trainer, and career and job search counselor for many years. Prior to joining the Harvard Business School, he was an independent outplacement consultant and trainer who did extensive work for Drake Beam & Morin. Earlier he held positions with Reo Hamel Associates; Nolan, Norton & Company; Data General Corporation; The Mitre Corporation; and the National Security Agency.

Gardella has also co-taught sessions on career management at Babson College and the Harvard Extension School. He has been a volunteer leader, speaker, and information source for Boston-area job-search support groups and has been active in the American Society of Training and Development, the Greater Boston Organizational Development Network, the International Association of Career Management Professionals, and the International Society for Performance Improvement.